The Communicatio

Personnel and PR Perspectives

The
Communications Challenge

Personnel and PR Perspectives

Edited by
Theon Wilkinson

Institute of Personnel Management

Phototypeset by James Jenkins Typesetting, London
and printed in Great Britain by
Dotesios Printers Ltd, Trowbridge, Wiltshire.

British Library Cataloguing Publication Data
The Communications Challenge
   1. Business firms, Management. Communication. Manuals
   I. Wilkinson, Theon
   658.4'5

   ISBN 0-85292-413-5

Contents

Acknowledgements   vi

Introduction:
    Overview of objectives   1
    A chapter of disasters   6

Part 1: Principles
    Truth and integrity   12
    Corporate and management attitudes   21
    Employee attitudes *(Wallace Bell)*   24
    TU role in communications *(John Monks)*   29

Part 2: Applications
    Methods   35
    Motivation for commitment   42
    Starting from scratch   48
    Changing with the times   51
    Crisis communication   56
    Sub-contractors dimension   68
    Public sector dimension   70
    European and international dimension
        (Jim Foulds and *Louis Mallet)*   77

Part 3: Examples of Good Practice
    Integrated communications philosophy *(IBM UK Ltd)*   86
    Company acquisitions *(MSAS Holdings Ltd* and
        Jardine Cargo Int.)   92
    Management buy-out *(Reedpack Ltd)*   95
    Relocation *(Digital Equipment Co)*   99
    Reorganization of field services
        (Digital Equipment Co)   103
    Major restructuring *(Courage Ltd)*   106

Conclusion   108

Acknowledgements

This book has been prepared under the auspices of the Institute's National Committee on Employee Relations by a working party composed of the following members:

Bob McLellan (chairman) – Plant Manager, Reed Corrugated Cases Ltd.

Shirley Bradley – Consultant and until recently Personnel Manager Kent Industrial Measurements Ltd

Howard Gibson – Manager of Personnel, Manufacturing and Development, IBM UK Ltd and since seconded to the Industrial Participation Association as Associate Director

Richard Holden – Personnel Director, Scottish & Newcastle Beer Production Ltd

Tony Lines – Personnel Manager – Luton, Vauxhall Motors Ltd

aided by

Julia Thorn a Director of Paragon Communications who was specially co-opted to provide a professional input from the public relations angle. Paragon Communications is one of the leading UK consultancies in the employee communications field and has won numerous awards from the Public Relations Consultants Association (including the Courage and Digital Equipment examples of good practice in section 3) and has held the Sword of Excellence Awards of the Institute of Public Relations in both 1987 and 1988 (including the MSAS Holdings example of good practice in section 3). The Institute of Personnel Management wishes to place on record its appreciation of Julia Thorn's very special personal contribution.

and edited by

Theon Wilkinson, Manager. Employee Relations, IPM

The Institute is particularly indebted for their personal contributions, to Wallace Bell, Secretary-General of the International Association for Financial Participation (formerly Director of the IPA) and to John Monks, Deputy General Secretary of the Trades Union Congress.

The book is the work of many people and has resulted from the support of a number of other committees within the Institute, notably the International Committee through their members Jim Foulds, Director, Group Personnel of DRG, and Louis Mallet, Personnel Manager Euro-Tunnel (UK) and the Public Sector Standing Committee in the respective chapters on their field of interest. Mention must also be made of Nigel Bain, Head of Communications at the IPM and a Council Member of the Institute of Public Relations, who was the main instigator of this publication at its conceptual stage and has used his dual role to ensure that it contains practical advice for students and managers in both the public relations and personnel field.

Introduction

Overview of Objectives

Communication – what does it mean? We all think we know but day-to-day experience with managers and employees alike indicates that the word is used in a number of different ways.

To the *Personnel Manager,* communication is a very wide term with a special employee relations dimension. It not only includes the dictionary definitions of 'giving, imparting, or exchanging of information, ideas, feelings etc to ensure others understand', and 'succeeding in conveying information' but also the methods used such as briefing, interviewing, counselling, employee reports as well as consultation and negotiation; each being sometimes mistaken as separate activities. Communication to the Personnel Manager is an all-embracing two-way process that requires very careful co-ordination by management of all the means of delivery, including those channels used in particular PR campaigns directed at employees.

To the *PR Manager,* communication is the planned and structured process of winning hearts and minds in order to influence opinion and achieve corporate objectives. In the context of employees, its prime aim is to create an environment which encourages employees to support the corporate mission and therefore understand the reasons for management decisions so they are more readily accepted and acted upon.

The quality and integrity of the message conveyed, whether by Personnel or PR, is critical to the successful continuance of the communication transaction.

A major research study[1] carried out in 1987 concerning the management of change and innovation in UK businesses revealed that senior executives put employee communications almost top of the list of criteria for success – second only to leadership – when asked to choose from a list of options that help facilitate progress in their own companies.

Encouraging stuff for those who believe in the importance of effective internal communications. Or is it? In the same survey, those very same executives – over 300 of them representing a range of businesses – put communications second to last (in order of priority) when asked initially to supply a 'top of the mind' unprompted response on the factors that aid change in companies in general.

Those findings seem to confirm that the problem of 'lip service' is still with us, clouding the commitment that actually exists to plan and implement employee communications programmes. When prompted, everyone acknowledges communication is an essential prerequisite of good business practice, but it barely gets a mention when managers decide, unprompted, what's important.

The survey highlights the challenge that faces both personnel and public relations professionals in fulfilling the needs of the organization, for they are in the 'people' business and communications is about people. It is about establishing a dialogue with people, providing them with information which they need and want. In order to gain a wider understanding of business objectives and support to achieve them, it also means listening and responding.

There is nothing altruistic about good communications – it is plain, hard-nosed commercial sense. At least that's the belief of some of Britain's most successful companies. For example, let us go back to that survey. It put ICI in the top five of all its league tables of perceived innovators in terms of business and people policies. And ICI's former chairman Sir John Harvey-Jones was one of only two businessmen to feature in a list of unprompted 'great leaders'. There he is at number four flanked by Churchill, Thatcher and Napoleon above him and Hitler, Kennedy, Montgomery, Jesus, Ghandi, De Gaulle and Michael Edwardes bringing up the rear. Interesting company. If nothing else, the list demonstrates the impact that Sir John has had in the business community with his open, and some would say, flamboyant style of business management.

His emphasis on the importance of communications is a key thread that runs through his book *Making it Happen*[2]. In it he says:

> 'Making it happen means involving the hearts and minds of those who have to execute and deliver. It cannot be said often enough that these are not the people at the top of the organization, but those at the bottom . . . With the best will in the world, and the best strategic direction in the world, nothing will happen unless everyone down the line understands what they are trying to achieve . . .'

The disciplines of personnel management and public relations have a vital role to play in achieving that aim.

Both disciplines suffer from misunderstandings and sometimes mutual antagonism – primarily the fault of individuals who fail to appreciate the full scope of their own function and lack of understanding of the other's. Personnel is sometimes characterized as being over-cautious, resulting in a communications void and PR can be regarded as insensitive to wider implications in its enthusiasm to create a 'good impression'. Both can be true – but there is no natural dichotomy between their respective objectives. It is only by working in co-operation that any gap that exists will be bridged.

The accord which should exist between the two is best illustrated by close examination of the definitions of both personnel management and public relations.

A recent definition of personnel management as agreed by the Institute of Personnel Management is:

> 'Personnel management is that part of management concerned with people at work and with their relationships within an organization. Its aim is to bring together and develop into an effective organization the men and women who make up an enterprise, enabling them to make their best contribution to its success.'[3]

The Institute of Public Relations has adopted the following definition of its craft:

> 'Public relations practice is the planned effort to establish and improve the degree of mutual understanding between an organization or individual, and any groups of persons or organizations, with the primary object of assisting that organization or individual to deserve, acquire and retain a good reputation.'

It is critical to understand that one of the prime 'groups of persons' that public relations aims to influence is a company's own employees. In fact, in most enlightened PR programmes employees are *the* most important audience, recognising that if a company does not have a 'good reputation' with its employees it will be an uphill struggle to convince anyone else of its merits.

Marks and Spencer is perhaps one of the most obvious examples of this philosophy in action. Communicating first and foremost with its own employees has given this company the confidence to describe its entire staff as members of its PR team.

How many other companies could credibly make such a claim? PR and Personnel working *together* to identify communications priorities and to ensure that presentation is interesting and relevant makes for a formidable combination.

As PR professionals Pat Bowman and Nigel Ellis say in their comprehensive publication:

> '. . . neglect of communications is a management failure allowing false ideas and distorted concepts to form and gain currency by default. Lack of communication, or inability to communicate clearly, is at the heart of a great deal of industrial unrest, job dissatisfaction and operational inefficiency. Good communication can contribute to more harmonious working relationships, understanding of commercial conditions, the acceptance of change and the improvement of productivity. It is not a panacea, but it is a vital part of good management.'[4]

They are equally clear in their endorsement of personnel and public relations working together to achieve the common aims of the business. There can be no dividing line, they say:

> 'Consultation and co-operation between the specialist functions of personnel and public relations is the only sensible way to meet the employee communication needs of an organization. However the two functions might be defined by management, together they share a responsibility for the communications link and for emphasizing the need for a policy of planned communication.'[4]

Of course, not all organizations have formalized personnel and public relations functions. But, whatever their size of structure, they should, at least, have a system to deal with personnel and PR issues; and the principle of employee communication being a prime feature of both remains constant.

Unquestionably, verbal one-to-one communication is the ultimate objective between the manager and the managed, and therefore communications within a small company should be easier than within large multi-site operations. But *should* doesn't necessarily mean that they are. What matters is the will to do so. The means of doing so becomes more complex the larger and more diverse the audience. But often the necessity for having formal channels to cope with complicated demands creates a discipline that is lacking in organizations where the managing director could, if he had the inclination, tell all employees personally what was happening in the business.

There are a number of golden rules for effective communication; the need to be regular, open, relevant, honest and to recognize the vital importance of the employees concerned being among the first to be told. How this all works out in practice is the crucial test.

The 'downside' of sophisticated communication channels, such as newspapers and videos that are being adopted increasingly by larger organizations, is that they can be allowed to replace the 'first line management' responsibilities to inform their subordinates of developments. In some cases management have absolved themselves of responsibility in deference to the monthly newspaper, for example. A recipe for disaster if management wants to demonstrate actively that it is managing.

There is no exact formula for effective employee communications and this book does not set out to provide one. What it does intend to achieve is a recognition of management's responsibility to involve employees in understanding the running of a range of organizations – large and small – through communication in its widest sense, and to provide guidelines on achieving an effective system.

Communication is, as defined in the opening paragraph, a two-way process encompassing telling, explaining, discussing, consulting and negotiating – a fact sometimes forgotten by zealous and often self-righteous organizations that bombard employees with information, yet fail to listen to responses. Establishing constructive feedback mechanisms that demonstrate that employees views are, at the very least, worthy of consideration, is often the most difficult part of the communications process. Employees views, at their best, provide rich veins of positive alternatives and reveal a highly motivated commitment to the primary aims of the business. Again there is no formula for success but we provide some principles.

Most of all this book is about Personnel and PR working together. It looks at communications from both perspectives and has been produced by professionals from both disciplines.

References

1 DELOITTE HASKINS AND SELLS (Management Consultancy Division). *The management challenge for the UK: a research study, 1987.*

2 HARVEY-JONES, SIR JOHN, *Making it happen: reflections on leadership.* London, Collins, 1988.

3 INSTITUTE OF PERSONNEL MANAGEMENT, *Code of professional practice in personnel management.* London, IPM, 1983.

4 BOWMAN P AND ELLIS N, *Manual of public relations*, 2nd ed. London, Heinemann, 1984.

A Chapter of Disasters

PR and Personnel not working together, or not aware of the need to integrate their separate communication functions, can cause havoc to employee morale on which so much of an organization's effectiveness depends.

There are significant differences in their roles which although complementary need to be identified and positively co-ordinated, else they run the danger of becoming confusing and divisive.

PR by its definition is primarily concerned with making an impact on the individual with information of a particular kind and in so doing is constantly seeking improved and innovative methods of direct communication.

Personnel management is also much concerned with individual communication but within the context of the organization as a whole and with the structured dissemination of all types of information up and down, through management and representative channels (where they exist) in a pre-arranged, and therefore more formalized situation.

Examples of how organizations can get their PR and Personnel roles at cross-purposes is given in the examples below. Some of these communication 'disasters' may be traced back to implementation inadequacies of Personnel, or over-enthusiasm of PR; some to an unfortunate combination of unforeseen events. Whatever the case, they illustrate the over-riding importance of getting their act together.

1   A large manufacturing company was engaged in the middle of crucial pay negotiations reported on daily by the media in which it was taking a very hard line to resist a claim for an additional 0.5 per cent on top of the amount already conceded, when a fanfare of PR news burst on the public with the announcement of a fantastic new process which would transform the profitability of the organization. The claim was promptly conceded!

The moral? It is essential to co-ordinate all public announcements, particularly in large corporations.

2   A manufacturer had to lay-off a significant number of its workforce because of the effects of a strike at a components supplier.

The personnel department decided to cancel the regular monthly newspaper the day it was due to print as 'there's no-one here to read it'.

After considerable persuasion they were convinced by PR of the merits of not only publishing the paper, but making it into a 'special' to explain the issues which had resulted in the lay-offs and mailing it to employees' homes.

A wave of sympathy for the striking components workers and latent hostility to their own employers was eased by the provision of 'the facts' in a format that had come to be regarded as credible and believable.

Subsequent research demonstrated that the employees appreciated the dilemma facing their own management. At a later date the unions were consulted on cost-cutting requirements and voted to keep the newspaper rather than the appropriate number of jobs the budget could fund.

The moral? Respond positively to new situations and discuss options with those concerned.

3   In the recent take-over battle for Rowntree it was reported in the national press that the company

> 'is planning a large-scale rationalization of its confectionary manufacturing facilities in both the UK and continental Europe. On some estimates, this could mean job losses running into thousands over a five-year period and ultimately savings to the company of up to £20m a year. . . . The news is likely to prove embarrassing to Rowntree on two counts: it has yet to inform unions of its intentions, and has built up a groundswell of support among shareholders based on its reputation as a caring employer. . . . Leaders of Rowntree's unions will today contact the company demanding details of any rationalization plans'.[1]

The moral? Make sure employees know your plans, at least at the same time, if not before public announcements.

4   In another takeover battle, this time between two multinational giants, the PR team in the UK organization had arranged for a most elaborate system of staged information with the news release scheduled for a fixed time in the afternoon, only to find that their dismayed staff first read of it in the *Evening Standard* during their lunch hour. The planners had overlooked the time difference between the headquarters of the two companies!

The moral? Meticulous timing of announcement is crucial to success.

5   A company which had grown into a major nationwide organiza-
     tion was planning to close its original factory from which it was
     founded. Redundancies were inevitable – but not for a year. It
     was anticipated there would be an 'emotional' response from
     the local media, even though it was to be a phased closure with
     the greatest assistance provided for all those affected.
        Personnel and PR worked closely together to devise a struc-
     tured internal and external announcement programme that
     would help to diffuse negative feeling and reassure employees
     on the efforts the company would be making over the next 12
     months to help them find alternative employment.
        On the day of the announcement employee briefings had
     been arranged for the morning and all external announcements
     to local media were to be released in the afternoon. A specialist
     media relations courier company had been supplied with the
     press releases which were sealed in envelopes marking the exact
     time of their distribution.
        The specialist company subcontracted the delivery task –
     without notifying Personnel or PR – and the new courier
     company erroneously delivered the releases in the morning.
        The organization in question had local radio playing on the
     shopfloor and headline news on the morning bulletin was the
     'shock' news that the factory was closing. The employee
     briefings had not yet started and there was understandable
     dismay and confusion amongst all staff.
        The moral? No matter how well you plan and co-ordinate a
     communications plan, remember it can always be ruined by the
     smallest player.
6   The personnel manager of an engineering company was helping
     to explain the significance of new work procedures linked to the
     planned introduction of an amended manufacturing process.
     Having invited 'any questions' he was asked an important but
     naïve query that had already been dealt with in the presenta-
     tion. He dismissed the question and asked if there were any
     'serious' questions that had not already been covered. There
     was complete silence and people left the meeting feeling con-
     fused and resentful. The new process led to a series of disputes
     and was never introduced. The personnel manager was later
     heard to say that progress was 'scotched by Bolshie shop floor
     attitudes'.
        The moral? Always encourage questions, however petty, as
     part of effective communications.
7   The personnel director in the service industry, proud of a new
     training scheme he had instigated, decided – against the advice

of PR consultants – to make public announcements about the skills and attitudes the scheme would instil in staff, before it had been tried and tested. Inevitably, the media concentrated on the worst aspects of the company's image when reporting on the new scheme and it became the focus of constant sniping every time there was an example of bad service.

The moral? Don't provide hostages to the future, stick to facts in the present.

8   A personnel department refused the offer of PR help in simplifying a staff handbook. The result was a comprehensive manual that had rules for every conceivable situation – but so incomprehensible that no-one could understand what they were.

The moral? Let the experts in on the act whenever possible.

9   A major company, operating in the food and drink sector, was considering the future of one of its smaller manufacturing sites. During the planning cycle it became clear that closure was a likely outcome of the review. Careful planning and preparation was taking place aimed at making an early announcement to the 50 employees affected. This process was brought to an abrupt halt when copies of the planning documents were stolen from the offices of a senior manager. The papers were then passed to a local MP who, in turn, forwarded them to the trade union with majority membership at the plant.

The result of this incident was to focus attention on the adverse media publicity which the company suffered as a result of the premature disclosure of information. The company appeared to its employees and to the outside world as underhand and untrustworthy. Much effort had to be expended by senior executives to win back the initiative, firstly with its own employees and secondly with the media.

In a company that prepared for 'every' eventuality, it was a shock to realise that the unforeseen could really happen.

The moral? Never be complacent about one's communication strategies. Events can easily overtake the best laid plans.

10 In an interview with the staff newspaper a militant shop steward of a company which was experiencing some industrial unrest described the managing director as a 'fascist'.

The personnel director picked up the comment on the proofs and insisted the comment was removed. The PR function which was responsible for the newspaper made a strong case for leaving the comments in on two main grounds:

1   The shop steward had been sought out for a comment and the credibility of the newspaper as an honest effective communications vehicle was in serious jeopardy if his views were subsequently doctored.

2 The comment was so offensive and irrational it was considered that few of his peers would wish to be associated with it.

The personnel director agreed to proceed with publication and the shop steward was swiftly 'sent to Coventry' by those he represented and a possible 'disaster' averted. A formal apology was sent by the union emphasising that the comment did not represent their view and giving an assurance that all discussions and negotiations would, in future, be conducted in a more constructive and mature fashion. This subsequently proved to be the case.

The moral? Honesty does pay – even when it may appear to be threatening.

11 A senior management training centre in the public sector, when launching a new training and development initiative, announced in the opening paragraph that its introduction would be phased in over a specific number of years 'on an age basis, commencing in 1988-89 with the following groups (grades specified) age 35 and under'.

The second paragraph set out to explain the details of the scheme and it was not until the final paragraph that there was a message of some reassurance for staff over the age limit:

'Any officers in these grades who are excluded from joining (the scheme) because of the age criteria, but who nonetheless require training or development should contact . . .'

As a result, the typical reaction to the communication from staff was 'if you haven't reached these grades by age 35, bad luck'.

The moral? Put the qualifying reassuring news up-front.

12 A major public sector trading organization, with a workforce of some 1,600 and a £90m annual turnover, sought to improve internal communications at all levels, by commissioning a detailed and searching survey through external consultants. The results of the survey were to be analysed and presented to the workforce in order to stimulate a review and initiate positive improvements.

The questionnaire covered such issues as the employees' knowledge of the company structure, market position and functions, their honest feelings about internal communications and their views on the organization in general. Officials of all recognized unions were involved from the outset and had approved the content of the questionnaire and arrangements for conducting the survey.

A standard question to elicit employees' general attitude to the organization was included. They were asked, 'If you were offered a similar job at a similar level of pay in another organization, would you be interested?'

Unfortunately, it had been overlooked that a recent external review had suggested that the company should consider putting its main handling function (currently carried out by in-house labour) out to tender. The management had strongly denied this was part of their strategy and had just about persuaded most employees of this and reassured them about security of employment, when they received this questionnaire which seemed designed to identify those individuals who could be made redundant and taken on by an outside contractor to run the service.

The result was total outrage – a blank refusal on the part of most employees to complete the form and overall it proved to be a totally unsatisfactory exercise. Trade union officials blamed management, management blamed the consultants and it took the organization backwards in internal relationships.

The moral? You cannot be too careful about the messages you give your workforce – however open and honest your motives.

Each of the above 'disasters' not only indicates a need for the management team with the PR and PM specialists to sit down together to agree a co-ordinated approach in advance and be ready to adapt it as the situation develops, but also to keep firmly in mind the prime importance of the integrity of the message.

References

1   WALLER D. *Financial Times*. May 1988.

1. *Principles*

Truth and Integrity

The Government's fight to ban the publication of Peter Wright's *Spycatcher* popularized a phrase in the English language which has become a euphemism for deliberately seeking to withhold all material facts. 'Economic with the truth' was a masterly phrase to disguise a less than forthright approach to 'the truth, the whole truth and nothing but the truth'.

It is a phrase that can accurately be applied to the internal communications' practices of many leading companies – and some would argue that a circumspect approach to the level of information supplied to employees is the safest route. For others, this apparent need for caution is a thinly veiled excuse for not communicating or only when pressed.

There are many arguments for and against complete honesty. Of course, there are legal restrictions imposed by the Stock Exchange on those companies whose shares are publicly traded that prevents them providing information 'material to its performance' that could be price 'sensitive' if it is not freely available to *all* shareholders. There is also the period of 'purdah' preceding the announcement of full-year and interim results when publicly quoted companies are forbidden to provide information that could lead to accusations of 'insider' trading. But with only about 3,000 companies listed on the full and junior markets, these constraints are not legitimate inhibitors to the free-flow of information for the vast majority of British companies. An organization is too easily caught out when it is being deliberately 'economical with the truth'. It is counter-productive and loses the confidence of one's audience when it is essential to maintain that confidence long-term.

The law, too, adds its weight and makes certain provisions for giving information to employees through Section 1 of the Employment Act of 1982 which imposes requirements on all registered companies that employ more than 250 people and who produce annual directors' reports. The Act stipulates that these reports should include 'a statement describing the action that has been taken during the financial year to introduce, maintain or develop arrangements aimed at . . .':

Communication

'providing employees systematically with information on matters of concern to them as employees'

Consultation

'consulting employees or their representatives on a regular basis so that views of employees can be taken into account in making decisions which are likely to affect their interests'

Financial Participation

'encouraging the involvement of employees in the company's performance through an employees' share scheme or by some other means'

Common Awareness

'achieving common awareness on the part of all employees of the financial and economic factors affecting the performance of the company'

That would appear to be an effective charter for galvanizing less than enthusiastic companies into action. But does the law work – and is there any positive action to ensure compliance? It would seem not. A survey conducted by the Institute of Directors in 1987 revealed that only 9 per cent of firms covered by the Act correctly fulfil these statutory obligations. What are the other 91 per cent doing, one wonders? And what effect is it having on the strength and efficiency of their businesses? The IPM, too, has been monitoring these reports for the last four years and in the most recent commentary expressed dismay at the increasing trend (+16%) to standard paragraphs which are now included in 56 per cent of the original sample, and deplored . . .

'the continued existence of a 'rump' of companies which appear to *either* ignore the statutory requirement altogether or claim exemption due to loopholes in the Act *or* publish very short and largely meaningless statements on 'policy' ignoring the requirement to provide a statement describing the 'action' that has been taken during the financial year.'[1]

The Introduction has already quoted Sir John Harvey-Jones' attitude to the contribution communication makes to business success. He has much to say in *Making it Happen* on the importance of two-way communication in general, and truth and integrity in particular. A selection of quotations under the following eight key headings demonstrate the philosophy that took ICI, under his chairmanship, from its disastrous slump in the seventies to its re-emergence as one of Britain's most successful and best-run companies:

1 Truthfulness and openness
2 Inclusiveness of information
3 Simplification of information
4 Setting the overall direction of an organization
5 Decision making
6 Initiation of action
7 Bad news/good news
8 External versus the internal perspective

Alongside these quotes are extracts from the IPM's own *Practical Participation and Involvement*[2] series which draw on a number of other management sources – notably the CBI and the Industrial Society – in emphasizing some of the points.

1 Truthfulness and openness

'. . . the organization which fails to make it happen is best characterized by a lack of truthfulness and openness. Truthfulness and openness without fear of the consequences is a most difficult trick within a large group of people. It is not that large outfits inevitably seek to recruit liars. It is a tribute, I suppose, to the English language that there are so many forms of circumlocution that it is remarkably easy to persuade yourself that you have made a bold statement, or conveyed the bad news, whilst in reality there is no conceivable possibility that the recipient has actually understood what you are talking about. Truthfulness in these circumstances really does mean ensuring that the point you are trying to get across has been received . . . There is a common idea that not revealing all the facts safeguards your power to manage your own affairs. The reality of course it that you are hampering your own chances of success, since information hoarding becomes a sort of group plague and in your own turn you will also lack the vital data you need to do your job.' (H-J)

'Once an organization has embarked on a communication programme, it needs to honour the "communication bargain" it has struck:

- good news as well as bad
- respond to requests for further information where confidentiality allows
- respond to criticisms and suggestions
- continue to communicate.' (IPM)

2 Inclusiveness of information

'Our forebears have given our company a tradition of open speaking and respect for differences of opinion which, in my view, is the most precious single inheritance that we have.' (H-J)

'. . . plain speaking and tolerance are tender flowers which have to be nurtured and helped to grow. One "hangover ridden" shortness of response, or a snappy turn-off to views you don't like, causes infinite harm. These understandable human reactions have to be channelled against the waffler, the apple polisher: the man or woman who by verbal skills seeks to evade taking a position, or in some cases actually saying anything at all.' (H-J)

'Employee participation and involvement plans and strategies should take as their starting point the high degree of common interest and mutual interdependence which must exist in any successful organization between the employer, the employees and their representative organization, the shareholder and, most significantly, the customer whom the organization seeks to serve.' (IPM)

3 Simplification of information

'We need to have simplified to a stage where one sentence; almost a slogan, will describe what we believe, and what we can accept and work to. This process of simplifying down involves attacking the "weasel words". We aim to make the simplifying process one of distillation and concentration rather than trying to make "umbrella" statements which are unobjectionable. We haggle and argue over single words. But we know when we have "got it", and when we have got it, we believe it and can work to it.' (H-J)

'It must be stressed that the two critical considerations which condition an employeee communication policy are:
1   that it is relevant
2   that it is capable of being understood
Employees will only be bored and mystified if too much information is presented in an incomprehensible style. That is the very opposite of what a good communication programme should seek to achieve.' (IPM)

'. . . our experience shows that if facts are to be believed and if those who give them are to be trusted, the information must be: REGULAR, not just at a time of crisis or in the context of annual negotiations. HONEST, the facts, both good and bad. OPEN to all employees, not just to management and representatives and with a chance to ask questions. RELEVANT, primarily about the local unit for which employees work and whose performance they can directly affect' (IS)[3]

4   Setting the overall direction of an organization

'One reason why you should try to develop the direction in which you think a company should go from both ends of the company at once is that in the process you gain commitment of those who will have to follow the direction – and "make it happen" – and in a free society you are unlikely to get this commitment without a high degree of involvement and understanding of both where the ultimate goal is and the process by which the decisions regarding the goal have been reached' (H-J)

'Our problems are, fundamentally, the need to achieve a common purpose within our companies and this requires British Managers to recognize what the CBI has described as "the alienated employee" . . . Thus, the fundamental emphasis of any participation and involvement programme should be on:
     increasing the profitability and success of the organization, for example, in adding value or in its measurable effectiveness
and
     increasing the sense of common purpose and motivating all employees to maximize their contribution by

endeavouring to gain their understanding of, and commitment and contribution to, the organization's success.' (IPM)

5 Decision making

'. . . if the right decisions are to be taken, it is essential that conflicting views are heard and thrashed out. The fact that you are up at the top of a business hierarchy does not confer all-seeing wisdom.' (H-J)

'The objective is to achieve . . . a more competitive, more efficient British industry through improved employer/ employee relationships by making sure that the decision-making in industry is with the understanding and, wherever practical, the acceptance of the employees involved.' (IPM)

'Whatever arrangements and procedures for participation may be established, managers remain responsible for making business and organization decisions falling within the area of their own accountability, and for communicating such decisions, with relevant background information, to employees.' (IPA/IPM)[4]

6 Initiation of action

'In a good organization, the objectives that have to be achieved are decided with considerable interaction between those who are going to carry them out, and those who ultimately have the responsibility for the leadership of the enterprise. This does not mean that objectives have to be liked. No organization likes being told it has to hold back its expansion or abandon some pet project. But first they have to understand why such an instruction is given, even when it appears to be against their interest, and secondly they have to have been involved in the decision and to understand and accept the consequences of such a strategic direction. They have to believe that there will be an advantage commensurate with, or greater than the sacrifice that they are going to make.' (H-J)

'Managers and supervisors must be held accountable for communicating with their own teams, with active board level commitment to providing information on a regular basis. This commitment must be permanent and seen to be so.' (CBI)[5]

'The Personnel function has a dynamic and innovatory role in developing employee communications. Personnel managers, in the words of the Code of Professional Practice recently published by the Institute of Personnel Management, have, amongst their responsibilities to their employer, to "encourage the development of effective consultation and communication at all levels in the organization" and, in their responsibility to employees, to "ensure that existing and potential employees are given full and accurate information concerning employment with their organization." It is therefore the responsibility of personnel managers to consider the extent and effectiveness of communication within their organization and propose, persuade and cajole line colleagues to take positive action where corporate communications are ineffective or non-existent. It will sometimes be difficult to obtain positive results and obtain top management commitment.' (IPM)

7 Bad news/good news

'Bad news in organizations is seldom received with much enthusiasm. The reality of life is, of course, that it is the bad news man who should be most prized. It is all too easy to get people who will tell you nice things, and after all there is not a lot you can do about that, but those who will stand up without fear or favour and tell you, hopefully tactfully, that things are not really the way that everybody else thinks they are, are pearls beyond price.

The most unhelpful position that a board of directors can take when a business is performing badly is to respond by saying that such a performance is unacceptable. It may be an absolutely true statement, but it does nothing whatever to give any guidance as to the ways in which performance may be improved and merely passes a message down the line that those at the top do not want to know the bad news and would like to dissociate themselves from it.' (H-J)

– and as a comment from the IPM working party:

First line managers rightly complain when they find themselves continually asked to pass on the bad news whilst they see senior management keeping the announcement of good news to themselves. An even distribution is not only fair, it is essential, as management divisiveness can undermine the communication process and message.

8 External versus the internal perspective

'The message that you are about to shut down a loss-making business may be very good news for your shareholders, or the financial analysts, but it is likely to be very bad news to the community in which you operate and to your employees. It may also be very bad news to the government of the country in which you operate. Yet all of them have to be communicated with, and persuaded that the steps you are taking are desirable and necessary, and will be carried out, bearing in mind the many different interests that are affected. This problem cannot be solved by blandness.

It is very tempting to try and avoid making any positive statements to anybody, hoping that "it will be all right on the night", but of course it never is, and you land in even deeper trouble'.(H-J)

'The needs of one's people are wider than just the pay packet. They wish to feel that they are doing a worthwhile job, which makes some contribution to society.' (H-J)

'In many companies, the co-ordination and administration of a comprehensive communication policy and programme will be the responsibility of the Personnel Department. The success of the programme will largely depend on the care and attention given to executing the policy and thus the personnel function will carry a heavy responsibility for its successful implementation.' (IPM)

References

1 INSTITUTE OF PERSONNEL MANAGEMENT. *Annual reports: employee involvement statement: the fourth year.* London, IPM, 1988.

2 INSTITUTE OF PERSONNEL MANAGEMENT. *Communication in practice.* (Practical Participation and Involvement Series, Vol. 1). London, IPM, 1981.

3 INDUSTRIAL SOCIETY. *Understanding the economic facts.* London, The Industrial Society, 1980.

4 INSTITUTE OF PERSONNEL MANAGEMENT AND INDUSTRIAL PARTICIPATION ASSOCIATION, *Employee involvement and participation code,* London, IPM/IPA, Rev. ed. 1985.

5 CONFEDERATION OF BRITISH INDUSTRY, *Guidelines for action on employee involvement,* London, CBI, 1979.

Corporate and Management Attitudes

The communication philosophy of any organization depends on a number of factors. The most important of these is the size of the organization, the resources employed and, to a large extent, the style of management – particularly its senior executives.

Not every organization can afford a specialist public relations department; indeed many small organizations cannot afford a personnel department. The responsibility for drawing up information briefs and ensuring that these reach the right people at the right time falls on the members of the management team; often the chief executive. In small organizations the information flow usually operates most sharply, through word of mouth. The management team recognize that employees get to know what is going on very quickly. They also know that they can add, change or correct information very quickly so that employees are never too far away from the management message.

There comes a point, as organizations develop and grow, when the need for a more structured approach to communications is apparent. Usually this starts with the need to communicate to a growing workforce where the task of collating and co-ordinating briefing material is transferred to the personnel manager. Parallel to this development, the organization often perceives the need to communicate more effectively with its customers and with the trade press. This external communication may be handled within the marketing function, perhaps by a publicity manager. These developments in internal and external communications set the pattern for the future as the organization continues to grow. This is where the 'communications challenge' originates.

This process of organizational development continues to the point where large organizations assign responsibility for communicating with customers, external agencies and employees to the marketing, public relations and personnel departments respectively. Some large organizations have moved on to create communication departments which focus on employee communication but also take in some public relations activities in areas such as the organization's relationship with the community.

This development, from small to large organizations, is set in the context of the organization's perceived need to communicate. The chief executive, at any stage of development, determines the resources to be employed in the communication process. Very often this is a reactionary pressure on the development of the communication process. If organizations have been less troubled by communication shortfalls then less resources will be employed to handle communications as a specific responsibility. If difficulties have been experienced in the past, it is likely that the chief executive will be persuaded to sanction more resources in the communication area.

Apart from size of organization and resources employed – both constraints on what can be done in the communication process – the real key lies in management style and its attitude to communication. A large organization, headed up by a personable individual who communicates well with the board of directors and runs a participative team will have an organization beneath them in which an open style of communication is the norm. The organization will benefit from the free flow of information both up and down the management chain. In such an open organization there exist clear demarcation lines for reponsibilities within the chain of communication, and senior executives know, usually without question, who is responsible for advising the outside world on developments within the organization. At the same time, those responsible for ensuring that the same information is made available to management and employees within the organization can get on with their task, and work to an agreed timescale which will ensure no embarrassment to either party.

This open style of communication can be contrasted to the organization that is so concerned with ensuring that no information leaks out before it is due to be released that, in many cases, employees first hear company news from external sources. Organizations that operate a 'closed' style of communication are quite common. Many would not recognize they are in this category for often their public face is at odds with reality. Such organizations are typified by managers who are reluctant to pass out information on company initiatives, product developments etc for discussion within the organization because they are concerned that the information will be mishandled or 'leaked'. Such fears may be well founded when the dissemination of information is not accepted as the norm. It is in this type of environment that the grapevine flourishes.

In any organization where people are seen to be important, management must make a substantial effort to ensure that communication works within the machinations of the structure. Communication will therefore be an integral part of all management training and a regular flow of information both up and down the structure will be accepted and necessary to the successful operation of the business. In an organization where people are kept 'in the know' their feeling of belonging and being involved will normally lead to loyalty and satisfaction with their jobs. This can often be seen in organizations with a very low labour turnover and which have many long-service employees. Good communication ranks high among the items which cause employees to feel well treated. In a recent survey it has been shown that money spent on communications such as newsheets, annual reports, weekly briefings etc often reaps as much benefit as money spent on canteens and other employee facilities. Many forward-looking organizations have proved that not only do managers need to be able to communicate, but, where open communication exists in its truest form, information and ideas flow up and down through the organization. Everyone is able to communicate if given the appropriate opportunity. This is used to best advantage in organizations where proper briefing systems, consultation, employee involvement, suggestion schemes and other such forums are encouraged and used as part of the everyday working environment. Management needs to be trained to make the most of these structures and to be able to offer the right information at the right time.

Clearly when information is being made available both within and outside the organization there must be a co-ordinated approach to ensure that the right people know at the right time. The vital rule must always be that nothing that impinges on employees goes out of the organization before it is known by everyone affected. Here one must rely on the interface between the personnel department and the public relations department. If these departments have clearly defined responsibilities and are working to a pre-agreed timetable there should be no difficulty in sharing information to achieve maximum impact both inside and outside the organization.

Should organizations be required to produce a policy statement on communication? As with so many key areas, good communication is fundamental to any organization and therefore some may question the need. But just as training and safety, for example, gain by publishing policy statements which focus attention on these issues and ensure that effective action occurs, so the publishing of policy statements, and all that goes with them, has proved equally germane in the communication area. Where this has not occurred, it is perhaps time that organizations take a long hard look at this fundamental aspect of their business objectives. It is more than a 'communications challenge', it is a business necessity.

Employee Attitudes

The previous chapter concentrated on the management's view of employee communication. This chapter focuses on the employees' view.

A joint TUC, CBI and ACAS exercise in 1987 produced a report on workplace communication among over 60 companies in the North of England[1] which revealed sharp contrasts between managements' and employees' views.

The evidence showed that while the great majority of managers (79%) considered their employees were kept well informed about matters that affected them at work, this was not the view shared by many employees.

In one company over half (56%), and in another nearly two-thirds (66%), did not think they were kept well informed on issues likely to affect them, and nearly three-quarters of all employee respondents believed that managers could communicate with them in a more effective manner. Hourly-paid employees were less impressed with efforts to keep them informed than their clerical colleagues.

Another survey[2] pointed to the same shortcomings of management communication. MORI (Market and Opinion Research International Ltd) has conducted employee surveys in more than 100 organizations over the last two decades, covering all aspects of communication, and has found that in replies to a standard question about half the typical workforce hold the view that their employer does not keep them fully, or even fairly well informed; and this pattern has shown only a marginal improvement over the last three years.

Clearly for many employees there is a communication gap. Wallace Bell – for many years Director of the Industrial Participation Association and currently Secretary-General of the International Association for Financial Participation – is an acknowledged authority on the subject. In the rest of this chapter he explores this problem and analyses employee attitudes.

'It's no use asking me, mate, I just work here.'

What it is that he, or she, does not know may be anything from the number of people employed on the site to what the firm's products are used for or what services it provides: anything at all outside the bounds of his or her immediate job, and the weekly or monthly pay packet. After nearly 20 years during which the principles of employee involvement and participation have become widely accepted by British management, and employee communications has developed into a growth industry, it may seem surprising that there are still very many employees who know little or nothing about their employer's business and, in general, appear not to be at all concerned about it.

They are to be found in three different settings. The first is in firms whose managements do not see any point in participation, which they regard as time wasting and interfering with the running of the business, and who do not think there is any reason for employees to be given more information than is necessary for the performance of their jobs. There are still many such firms in Britain today, and there are subsidiary units in larger, and perhaps more participative organizations, whose managements have, and want to preserve, the same 'them and us' attitudes: 'We are here to manage; they are paid to do as we tell them.'

The second setting is in organizations that do believe in employee communications, and may spend a great deal of time and money on them, but it has little effect on the employees. Somehow, management seems to have got its communications wrong.

The third is in firms where communications are in general good, and appreciated by many employees, but others are simply not interested. There are always some employees who want only to come to work, do their job, get paid, and go home. They do not want any involvement beyond that.

Macho-management

There is not much that can be done to improve things in the first setting – the 'macho-management' firms – especially if they are independent businesses. Many are relatively small firms whose managements are quite immune to the advocacy of more enlightened employment policies by the IPM and other bodies. Moreover there is no real evidence that employees in such firms are dissatisfied with their lot. They are often either young, short-term employees who move from job to job and have no real interest in what firm they work for, or are in the 'come to work . . . and go home' category. It is often the case that managers attract the kind of employees who fit in with their particular management style.

There may, however, be considerable frustration in the subsidiary unit of a larger organization if a new managing director

whose style is authoritarian follows one who had established good
employee communications and involvement practices. I have seen
years of painstaking effort to develop effective participation
destroyed almost overnight when it became obvious that the new
man at the top had no commitment to it. The resultant cynicism
among the workforce is very hard to overcome.

Good intentions

What of the second case, the well intentioned management that puts
a lot of effort into employee communications but to little avail? The
trouble here is often that management has decided what they think
employees should know, or should want to know, but have not
actually found out what, in reality, they do want to know. The
predictable result is over-kill: flooding employees with masses and
masses of information, often in a form that is quite indigestible to
the majority. It is certainly desirable that everyone in the organization should be provided with some information about its
performance, but I have sat through many a video of a company's
annual results that threw figure after figure on to the screen, and
piechart after piechart, that could not be understood, let alone
remembered, even by staff in the corporate finance department.
With that kind of presentation, people simply switch off and think
about something else.

The problem is with both content and presentation. There are
some things – relatively few – that employees must know in order to
do their jobs. They are mainly specific, and related to the
employees' immediate work area, or even to one particular job.
There should not be any major problem in communicating this
information, and getting it accepted and understood, as it concerns
things that employees *do* want to know, although they may not be
at all interested in comparable information concerning other
people's jobs. The communication is therefore likely to be less
effective if information about many different jobs is included in the
same package.

Then there are things that it may not be essential that employees
must know, but desirable that they should. Some are specific – how
their own jobs relate to other parts of the organization – some are
more general, and concern the business as a whole. This is where
many communication systems break down, and although information is provided it is not received; employees hear what is said,
but it does not catch their attention and is not assimilated in their
minds. In order to be received, information should be as simple as

possible, and not contain too many details. Most employees are interested, or prepared to be interested, in how their own jobs fit into a wider context, but there is a rule of thumb that is often forgotten – their interest is in inverse proportion to the distance from their own jobs – so the simplicity of information should be in direct proportion to its distance from the workplace. But often it is information about the business as a whole that is presented in most detail and in the most elaborate form.

One reason is perhaps that today's more enlightened managers have come to believe that employees should be provided with full information about almost every aspect of the business, and apart from strictly confidential matters, nothing should be hidden from them. As a result, they tend to provide far more information than most employees can possibly absorb, and their communications packages are full of indigestible facts and figures.

Their mistake is not in openness – in being willing to give out information – it is in thinking that they must actually provide it in full to everyone – almost thrusting it on them – rather than ensuring that everyone knows that it is available if they want it. Availability is the key. Employees or their representatives – those who are interested – should know that they can get further information on matters that are not included, or not detailed in more general communications, simply by asking for it; and that if they ask questions they will get honest answers, and will not be blamed for having asked.

With careful regard, therefore, to what information employees at different levels actually want and will respond to, and in what form they can most easily assimilate it, communications in many companies could become much more effective.

You can't win them all

Even in firms with the best communications, however, there will always be some, and often many, employees who are not interested in anything except their own jobs and their pay packets, and who will not respond to anything in a wider context. Well, you can't win them all. But in some cases it may be that they just do not see any connection between the information provided about the business as a whole, and their own place in it. It is not only remote, to them it seems irrelevant. What does a profit of £100 million mean to a shop assistant or a part-time packer earning £100 per week?

They are of course wrong. The health and progress of the firm they work for is very important to their job security and future pay packets, but unless they can see an immediate and direct connection, their attitude is understandable. But this is where financial participation –

profit sharing and employee shareholding – can help to change things. I think it is significant that Section 1 of the Employment Act 1982 requiring companies to include employee involvement statements in their annual reports puts financial participation: 'encouraging the involvement of employees in the company's performance through an employees' share scheme or by some other means', before 'achieving a common awareness on the part of all employees of the financial and economic factors affecting the performance of the company'. If employees know that the profit figures will be reflected in their bonuses, and the growth and success of the company will influence the value of the shares they hold in it, they are much more likely to be interested in the business results. As one managing director said at an IPA conference, 'It really is rather silly talking to employees about profit, if they don't get any of it'.

The bad news

Communications in any organization, however participative, come under the greatest strain when the news is really bad. It is easy to say that employees want to hear only the good news, not the bad. In fact they will usually accept the bad news if they have been prepared for it in advance. What they do not want is the shock of really bad news – closures and redundancies – being suddenly sprung on them without warning when everything that has gone before has seemed encouraging. This poses one of the most difficult questions for management – when to tell?

There is no easy answer, and many arguments can be put forward for not making any 'premature' announcement. Nevertheless good employee communications depend to a large extent on trust. But trust is not a management prerogative; it has to be earned. It may take months, even years to establish, but it can be destroyed in minutes. Trust does not mean that everyone will like what they are told, but it does imply an acceptance that management are being honest in what they say, and are not hiding the things they do not want people to know.

No one has said that employee communications are easy!

References

1   TUC, CBI and ACAS. *Working together – the way ahead: workplace communication and employee involvement in Yorkshire and Humberside.* London, TUC/CBI/ACAS, 1987.
2   STUBBS R. *The total communicator* (a conference paper). London, MORI, May, 1988.

Trade Union Role
In Communications

John Monks, Deputy General Secretary of the TUC

My first lesson in the importance of communicating effectively in the trade union world was given by a shop steward who was a member of the Communist Party. At my first branch meeting, I had spoken on a subject with more enthusiasm than knowledge and contributed to a decision, opposed by the branch executive, which subsequently had the serious effect of worsening relations with the local full-time officer. At the end of the meeting, the shop steward took me on one side and said 'Be constructive, read Citrine or Hannington on the conduct of meetings, polish your public speaking and then maybe you'll make a useful member of this union!'

Initial annoyance at the criticism gave way to curiosity and I followed that advice, reading Citrine on chairmanship, the Labour Party booklet on public speaking (both of which, incidentally, are still available), attending weekend schools and watching, with rather more respect, how some of the more experienced members of the branch performed. I am still conscious of a debt of gratitude to that shop steward.

In the late 1960s in the union world – the time of that experience – communications depended on the ability to write an accurate minute, pen a clear letter and perhaps above all, to address a range of audiences including mass meetings of members, negotiations with employers, and meetings of tripartite committees involving civil servants, employers and the wider community.

Effective communication has always been an essential skill of the trade union organiser and negotiator. Unions were, and are, built by people. People – where a union is not already recognised – with the ability to persuade workers to take a chance. Joining a union was, and is, regarded by a significant number of employers as an unfriendly act, possibly leaving the worker open to retaliation or victimization. A worker joining a union in these circumstances is taking a risk and it requires considerable skill and ability on the part of a union organiser to persuade workers that it is in their interests to join.

Similarly in negotiations and in representations on behalf of individuals, union officials are continuously engaged in the difficult act of persuasion; sometimes persuading people to be bold enough to support a challenge to their employer and at other times, persuading people that it's time to settle a deeply held difference. By and large, unions do not have the power to command, they only have the ability to persuade and cajole.

It could be said, therefore, that unions have always been in the communications business. However, what has been changing rapidly is the sophistication and methods of communications used by employers and government – changes which unions have found it increasingly necessary to match. This chapter looks at what has been occurring and assesses the union response.

Because British industrial relations have developed without any overall pattern being evident, it is always dangerous to generalize. Practices vary greatly according to the styles and traditions of industries, the nature of the product or service, and the grade of workers concerned. The company's country of origin can also be an important factor.

Nonetheless, it is commonly recognized that many managements now place greater emphasis on using new communications techniques to win commitment and support from their employees than was, perhaps, the case prior to this decade. The reasons for this, again, are generally accepted.

The serious economic collapse of 1979-81 and the thousands of company closures or rundowns, and the millions of resulting redundancies brought home to some managements, not already alert to it, the fact that there are advantages to management of informing employees directly on matters likely to affect their interests. The tactic, popularized in management by Michael Edwardes at British Leyland (BL), of writing directly to every worker setting out the company's view, and in so doing bypassing the extensive shop steward organization, bred many imitators.

Hitherto the practice had developed in many of the unionized plants of British industry of communicating and discussing key policy changes with trade union representatives who in turn passed on information to their members. This 'single channel' of information, consultation and representation reflected union wishes. It also reflected the fact that, as line managers are not always responsible for communication, management left it to unions to put over information on issues relevant to employees. In effect the responsibility for communication rested with shop stewards – a responsibility which was jealously guarded once it had become established by custom and practice. In some cases it was ratified by formal agreements.

At a recent talk at the London Business School to some largely young MBS students, I was tackled about this by a disbelieving questioner, 'How could managers be so stupid as to allow this?' In fact they were not stupid. It was a practice which recognized that collective bargaining had not only become the main means of determining pay and other basic conditions of employment, but in the 1960s and 1970s, its scope had widened to embrace other topics. Shop stewards were often seen by managements and union officials as key players in industrial relations. It was believed – rightly in many cases – that they were able to rely on a fierce loyalty from their constituent members – a loyalty which did not rest on union rules or on the terms of collective agreements. To bypass them was to cause trouble.

Again generalizations are dangerous. There were employers who never conceded the 'single channel'. According to the Workplace Industrial Relations Survey, even in strongly organized workplaces, consultative arrangements as distinct from collective bargaining channels, survived much more vigorously than had been thought at the time of the Donovan Commission, and the existence of a strong trade union organization did not inevitably undermine such practices. But the recession of 1979-81 did allow employers to try new approaches and many were very ready to shower individual workers with the 'bad news' without much regard for custom and practice or the displeasure of the shop stewards. (Companies are usually far readier to communicate 'bad' news rather than 'good' since the latter might of course increase workers' expectations about rewards). A range of measures have been used including direct letters to employees, company newspapers, videos, team briefings, and quality circles.

Less common but even more noticeable to unions has been the way in which employers have actively pursued communication and media strategies in industrial disputes with the aim of influencing the workers on strike and, if possible, their spouses and families too. BL were a spectacular example of this but it was also used extensively by British Coal and the Government during the 1984/85 NUM strike and most recently by P&O in their dispute with the NUS centred on Dover. Extensive campaigns were waged in attempts to engage in a tug of war with the union concerned for the loyalty and commitment of the workers.

But it would be quite wrong to think that these changes in management's favour have solved management's communication problem. While it may be unrealistic for shop stewards in many companies to believe in returning to the position of hearing information about company intention direct from senior management well before middle and junior management, a communication strategy aimed to bypass unions is unlikely to work in the longer term.

Intelligent communication is based on a recognition that interests within an employing unit often conflict and that management information, based as it is on management objectives, is likely to be treated with sceptism. If additionally it is used dishonestly, cynically, or incompetently, its credibility, and that of its authors and sponsors, will be damaged.

Nor is a management likely to benefit from the top down communication system alone – in effect telling its employees what to do. What will benefit an intelligent management, is a system which provides a chance for them to listen. Listening improves the quality of leadership. By reaching an understanding on communications with the recognized union, or unions, management will generate respect for the quality, reliability and consistency of the information.

This argues strongly for trade union representatives to become essential links in the communication process and involve them fully in discussion and consultation at an early stage. This in turn should help lead to joint consideration of problems. Good and respected communications methods and systems are an essential base for good relationships; indeed, it is impossible to envisage the latter without the former.

Yet the question of communication channels remains a live issue with a range of conflicting views. On the one hand, the current wish of Ministers in the Department of Employment is for employers to make collective bargaining and unions irrelevant by dealing directly with individual employees. This has supporters among some managements. It is also an objective of many of those advocating human resources management which aims to control closely the commitment, training, payment, monitoring and advancement (or otherwise) of workers.

On the other hand, there are pressures within the context of the Single European Market and 1992 for Britain to move closer towards Continental systems of which a statute based works council is usually the cornerstone. In the European context, works councils have statutory rights to information, consultation and representation which, particularly as far as future company policy is concerned, go well beyond those established in collective agreements in Britain. The concept of works councils has long been viewed with scepticism by British unions but there are signs of a relaxation of attitudes and a willingness to, at least, look afresh at it.

At some stage soon there are likely to be clashes at the European

Community level about the incompatibility of the UK Government's views with those of most other Community members and no manager should be sanguine that Britain can remain aloof from key European practices.

More immediately, however, managements have to ask themselves whether, because human resource management has been successful in, say, IBM and some Japanese companies, it is capable of the kind of universal application that Government Ministers seem to believe.

Managements would be well advised to be cautious. While many of the features of human resource development are good management practices thoroughly applied, it is evident that for it to work in a way which keeps the union out requires a number of features:

- a steadily growing market making it possible to absorb employees displaced by productivity gains in new activities – few HRD non-union systems can withstand significant redundancy:
- considerable investment in well trained managers, and ready access to substantial training facilities – HRD is very expensive;
- a consistent ability to pay above the union rate.

The fact is that few companies can demonstrate all three of the above features, or at least sustain such features. Any moves to make British industry more efficient and competitive, to improve training and erase this country's dismal record in this respect, and to show a proper regard for the individual at work, are to be welcomed. But it must be recognised by managements that unions cannot be eradicated by HRD methods, and it is foolish for them to be adopted with this objective in mind.

One example should illustrate this. One of the elements of HRD – performance related pay – is currently being promoted as a means of transferring pay negotiation to the employer and the individual worker – away from the union area. But, in essence, how novel is this concept? It was the piecework system – one form of performance related pay – which gave rise to shop stewards and to plant bargaining. Piecework generated arguments about performance criteria, consistency of management decisions, and allocation of easy or difficult or unpleasant jobs. It has its advantages, particularly in terms of motivation, but also its disadvantages in terms of work relations. The newer systems of performance related pay raise at least some of the same problems as piecework. The role of the union tilts towards seeking to agree criteria and the price for achieving these, and then to aim for their consistent application. The union role changes, but it's not diminished.

All these developments pose challenges to unions. The union role may, however, diminish if there is a slowness to adapt. These changes in management practices are occurring at the same time as Government legislation is pressing hard on unions, and raising big questions about their communication strategies.

The legislative pressure was first experienced in 1984 by the Trade Union Act which introduced the provision requiring unions with political funds to conduct a ballot of all members as to whether the fund should be retained. This legal requirement was a major challenge to unions' administrative and communications systems – particularly those without computerized, direct mailing facilities. After considerable efforts, all unions comfortably won their ballots to retain their political funds but unions had to find ways of communicating with members who did not go to branch meetings.

That was just the start of further legislative moves on balloting by the Government. Also under the 1984 Act, secret individual balloting was introduced both prior to industrial action and for executive elections. Central registers of members had to be compiled. The 1988 Employment Act extends the balloting provision particularly to the election of general secretaries and presidents.

Some unions already had extensive experience of conducting ballots and of operating very large computerized mailings. But many did not, and the effect has been to prompt those unions to look beyond their activist minority to seek commitment and support from all members. This in turn has increased union interest in new communication techniques and generated the use of polling, advertising and video. It has led to a marked improvement in union journals. Many unions are much more conscious of image, and alert to the skills of the public relations consultant. The TUC has issued guidance to unions in this area and is greatly developing its own work in promoting trade unionism through the use of outside advisers.

So the new-found interest in communications is proving both a challenge and an opportunity to unions, as well as to managements. It will be important to keep it in perspective and not let the enthusiasm of the experts distort the essential features of good industrial relations – respect, commitment, straight dealing, intelligence, sympathy and relevance to the ordinary worker. But communications skills and techniques are likely to feature more rather than less, and none of the institutions concerned in industrial relations can afford to ignore them.

2. *Applications*

Methods

Giving people information is *not* communicating.

An organization truly committed to the principle of involving employees in the running and future direction of the business, might circulate to all employees the minutes of every single meeting held. It would certainly be taking a course that was honest and open – but experience shows that it is more likely to be creating a waste paper problem than a solution to the communications need.

People are interested in what is *relevant and understandable to them.* Some may say that's patronizing. It's not. It is a simple fact of life that every good communicator recognizes – be they a lecturer who enthuses his students, a politician who gets voted into office or a businessman who motivates his employees to successful performance.

Knowing *how* to communicate and the most effective channels to employ, is just as important to the end result as *what* you tell people.

Management bears the principal responsibility for communicating with employees and on each occasion needs to consider the audience, the message and in relation to one another, the method, and whether by using the personnel department and/or the specialist skills and techniques of PR they are more likely to get the message across.

A personnel professional was heard to describe PR as 'the sizzle on the sausage'. It was intended to be a criticism, inferring all gloss and no substance. But who would be tempted to eat a cold, congealed sausage – unless of course they were very hungry?

Communications techniques have reached a stage of advanced sophistication – yet all relevant research shows that the preferred source of information among employees is face-to-face with management.

That would be fine if all managers shared the same high level of communications skills; if companies could and would devote a large proportion of time to ensuring that managers were in full possession of all the facts and had the time and confidence to pass them on and field queries; if all managers interpreted those facts in the same manner without taking account of their own position and interests; and if employees could absorb and remember information presented verbally. These are the criteria for success if heavy reliance is placed on face-to-face communications. But, of course, it is highly unlikely that all will be met. So although face-to-face is a vital and integral part of the communications mix, and one to be encouraged and nurtured, there has to be the means to ensure consistency and discipline in the communications process if all employees are to get the same message, at the same time in a manner which engages their interests and promotes understanding. And that is where formal channels and techniques come in.

The need for this disciplined approach to communication is recognized by many organizations, and the larger they are, the greater the control mechanism, as the following typical information memorandum at IBM shows:

Plant Management Announcement

Please arrange to release the following information in accordance with the schedule:

Distribution 'A'	on completion of sign off
Affected managers	at functional managers' discretion
Non-affected managers and affected staff	1330 Tuesday 9 August 1988
General release and notice boards	1400 Tuesday 9 August 1988

The relevance of the information, in this case a staff appointment, to a particular group has been identified and a policy put into practice to ensure those most concerned receive the news before general release and through the most appropriate channel.

The success of all channels inevitably depends, to a large extent, on fulfilling the 'it's not *what* you do it's the *way* you do it' factor. Personnel may well influence the 'what' while PR has the experience to mould the 'way'. The following is a round-up of some of the techniques available to management. All have varying strengths and weaknesses which are outlined. Determining and implementing a combination to suit the nature of the material and the needs of the audience is the challenge of effective communications.

Face-to-face. be it through individual or group briefings, is pre-ferred, and offers potential for immediate feedback but can suffer from inconsistency and indiscipline unless controlled. As this is the key method, a more detailed commentary on it is given later in the chapter.

Letters are personal and direct but can lack impact and readability, unless confined to crisis situations when the message, literally, needs to be brought home.

Electronic mail is being used increasingly by those companies with the appropriate equipment, as a direct and immediate form of communication. It is best used for facts that need to be communicated quickly.

Publications produced on a regular basis are popular and readable – if professionally produced – and enable employees to absorb information at their own pace either at work, or away from the workplace when their families can be included. The combination of news and feature coverage makes publications effective for putting developments into perspective with in-depth background articles. They can infer independence and encourage feedback, but can be relatively costly, particularly for small groups of people.

Typewritten news bulletins can be swift and cost-effective but restrict the depth and background that can be provided. Unless there is the facility to reproduce photographs or illustrations they can also lack impact and readability.

Annual reports for employees can channel information of special relevance and interest to employees in relation to financial per-formance. Many Plcs distribute the shareholders' annual report to staff, particularly as more employees become shareholders in their own right. Since those who are shareholders are entitled to receive the official report, providing it for everyone avoids creating dual population problems.

Management instruction memoranda can be important in staging the information and ensuring that all the various levels of manage-ment are in the picture before the relevant staff and the public (when appropriate) are informed.

Video and AV can have power and impact, and are ideal to support face-to-face presentations, but absorption of complicated information presented in televisual form alone, is limited. Experience has shown that presentations by a senior manager are generally much better received than those by an actor or media personality, although a personality can be used effectively to interview management. Videos are effective 'scene setters' with detailed information provided in printed format. Cost can be significant, averaging from £1,000 per minute, and the equipment necessary to show video is also a cost and logistic constraint. Interactive videos are being used increasingly for training purposes.

Audio-cassettes are effective for employees who spend part of their working day in vehicles fitted with the necessary equipment – but of limited relevance to others. They can provide an alternative 'personalized' form of contact for those who cannot have regular face-to-face briefings, but would need some 'hard copy' support material if detailed information needs to be assimilated and remembered. Like televisual methods, they are best used as 'scene setters'.

Notice boards can be an effective focal point if they are accessible and effort is devoted to their presentation and topicality. They cannot be relied upon as a sole source of information as it is impossible to guarantee that employees will look at them. It is a passive form of management communication that places the onus on employees. They are good as back-up or for information that employees may *want* to know, rather than *need* to know.

The telephone is the mainstay of direct, everyday communication and it can also be given wider relevance with recorded news updates and answerphone feedback facilities, though the adverse reactions to recorded messages shold be remembered. Many people regard them as poor substitutes for the real thing.

Viewdata is immediate and quick but lacks impact and readability and, obviously requires a networked system and ready access for all employees. It is useful for the swift dissemination of facts employees need to know but inappropriate for background or positioning.

Electronic notice boards can be useful focal points in environments where there is a large concentration of employees such as on a factory shop floor. The amount of information they can convey is generally limited, and it can also be distracting.

Posters and wallcharts can attract attention, but the amount of information that can effectively be conveyed is limited. They can best be used as 'memory joggers' for particular campaigns.

In-house radio has been used by some companies to great effect but it is distracting and therefore, where this is undesirable – inappropriate. It can be very 'big brotherish' if used purely for company information and is best used as a motivational form of entertainment providing information in a subtle manner.

Local independent media is important to large single-site operations as employees are part of a community as well as part of the company, but direct control of coverage is limited. Corporate campaigns run in conjunction with the local paper or radio can help to generate pride among employees.

National press and media can be of vital importance in special circumstances, especially for the larger corporate organizations. Employees should never learn of company developments that have a direct relevance to them from the local or national media. If common courtesy doesn't dictate this course, then good business practice should.

The mix of methods in relation to the message and the audience will vary from one organization to another, depending on their size, management style and special circumstances; likewise the degree of involvement of Personnel and PR. The responsibility will, however, always remain with management and whatever techniques are used they should be seen, as far as information to employees is concerned, as only backing-up the essential face-to-face communication with the individual or small group.

Getting the message across (face-to-face) and two-way flow

However conscientiously management endeavour to communicate through line management or supervision, there is always the danger of a filtering or alteration of the information that is passed down.

Senior management needs to set up procedures, either formal or informal (or both), to check that all desired information is permeating through the system to the individual employee, to the union and/or staff representatives where appropriate and to the different levels of management.

Whatever system is selected, management need to operate in a genuinely open and non-critical environment. Ideally, problems or failures in downward communication should not be dealt with harshly or resentments may build up.

Formal

Staff consultative meetings with two-way information and question sessions, including topics which should have been disseminated since the last meeting, are a means of checking on, and confirming knowledge levels.

Brief departmental/sectional meetings for passing on information are also useful at regular intervals. These should be treated as important and 'pressure of work' not used as an excuse for cancellation. Managers and supervisors should have a simple agenda of the information they are supposed to pass on and they should genuinely welcome questions. In some companies it can be beneficial for senior managers to attend these meetings from time-to-time, provided they can avoid participating too much and dominating them.

Informal

Some senior managers find that inviting a cross-section of staff to coffee or 'beer and sandwich' sessions allows for a relaxed two-way flow of information.

Managers who can arrange to spend time on the shop floor should chat to operators and junior staff. Again, this requires considerable effort to build up a correct climate and avoid line management and union suspicion.

Communication Surveys

Companies can invest considerably in communication activities and yet be shocked and saddened that the information fails to reach all levels of staff. Senior management need to arrange their own spot-checking system in a sensitive and consistent manner to ensure that all members of staff have heard or read, and understood the issued information.

IBM carry out their own surveys at two or three yearly intervals to ascertain their employees' view on the best sources for different types of information (see table of questionnaire results on page 90).

The relevance of statistics from any one company, however, has to be treated with some circumspection as it relates to sources that the organization are using and gives no indication of others that may be appropriate.

Attitude Surveys

The importance of checking on the amount and quality of the information reaching the employee comes through repeatedly in commentaries on successful company practice. Many organizations today go to considerable lengths to conduct regular attitude surveys, usually through an external agency, to sharpen perceptions on what employees need information about, to check on morale indicators and to assess the value-for-money of the various communications methods being used. Examples have been quoted from surveys by ACAS and MORI to show the disparities between management and employee attitudes to the effectiveness of communication. This is a world-wide problem and not confined to the UK, as similar surveys conducted by the US Labour Relations Institute in North and South America, show. Managers are, therefore, faced with the challenge of bridging this gap between the organization's needs and employees' needs and, at the same time, of paying more attention to the evidence of disparity between them.

Attitude surveys, repeated at regular intervals, are one of the most useful tools. An independent consultancy specializing in such surveys, carried out an assignment among managers in a large multi-site organization in 1985, and again in 1987[1]. The purpose was to ascertain managers' views on pay and benefits but, in the section on communications, a question was slipped in about their opinion of this kind of questionnaire. The range of responses on the first occasion revealed only a general and uneven support but after the second survey it was possible to use the results as a definite morale indicator with support rising significantly in each of the twelve sites except one which remained stubbornly low. A morale problem on this one site was immediately highlighted and management were able to take appropriate corrective action.

References

1. EPIC Industrial Communications Ltd.

Motivation for Commitment

	% agreement	
		Trade
	Managers	_Unionists_
Increasing the commitment and involvement of employees will be the primary issue of the 1990s	79	55
Most managements recognize that improving employees' motivation will be a top priority in the 1990s	77	48

The results above form part of the recent EPIC Industrial Relations Opinion Survey[1] which was completed by 292 managers and 291 trade unionists (all of whom are actively involved in industrial relations) together with 34 academics and commentators – a total of 617 respondents.

The results suggest that 'motivation' and 'commitment' are going to be major concerns for management over the next ten years with four out of five managers, and half the trade unionists agreeing that 'increasing the commitment and involvement of employees will be the primary issue of the 1990s', and that 'improving employees' motivation will be a top priority in the 1990's. The significance of this for PR and personnel managers goes without saying.

The success of an internal communication policy depends on a series of separate and distinct motivators. These can be considered under the following five headings:

1 Carrying out the job
2 Understanding the business
3 Pride in the business
4 Participating in the business
5 Caring communications

1 Carrying out the job

The first priority for a systematic communications programme, as stated in the Institute's *Practical Participation and Involvement* series, is to meet the employees' *felt* needs for information directly relevant to their job. (A number of surveys have shown that employees' *stated* needs are primarily for information that directly affects them.)

Typically, the employees' felt needs for information include the following details:

the job
- the operating details
- the personal performance standards required
- the quality of 'product' standards required
- the relationship with other jobs in the same area
- the details of the overall process
- the likelihood of technological change
- the outside market; raw materials, customers, etc.

pay and prospects
- the details of pay and how determined
- procedure for overtime, holidays, sickness
- prospects, security, promotion, internal transfers, etc.

physical needs
- personal safety, protective clothing
- canteen facilities
- factory layout, first-aid, counselling, car-parking

l/6,1
relationships
- with the boss and 'grandfather' boss
- with work colleagues
- with employee representatives as appropriate; trade unions, safety representatives, etc.

The responsibility for ensuring these information needs are met and regularly updated falls to management with the support of the personnel and PR functions as seems appropriate. The employee's immediate 'boss' might discuss the job and the relationships, the personnel officer the pay and physical needs, while the PR staff might be involved in preparing an induction programme with an employee handbook – all co-ordinated by management.

The potential benefits to the organization from meeting the employees' felt needs for information are not only measured in terms of job performance but, by clearly attempting to identify with their needs, employees in turn are likely to be more receptive to what the organization needs them to know and understand.

2 Understanding the business

The second priority – having established confidence in job information needs – is to increase the scope of employees' interest in information less obviously relevant, but important for an understanding of the business as a whole.

The results of surveys which show that employees are only marginally interested in the organization outside their main area of work are not surprising, considering that many employees remain ignorant of what information is available. Such information includes:

quality
- customers' particular requirements
- customers' complaints

management data
- management accounts
- production control

commercial
- the changing commercial position of the organization
- competitors' progress

productivity
- actual against target
- plans for improvement
- competitors

financial
- an understanding of the economic facts of life
- the position of the organization
- changes outside the organization which will affect it

Many of the above concepts are quite complex and the communicator – whether management, personnel, PR or a combination of all three – will often need to educate the recipients of the information before they can take it in.

The potential benefits to the organization from this form of horizon-enlarging information is the development of trust in the integrity of management communications – very important and particularly so in times of crisis; an increased awareness of the constraints on the organization stimulating an interest in cost-saving and productivity; and the recognition of the manager's contribution to the success of the organization.

3 Pride in the business

Success breeds pride and pride in the business generates further success. Pride in the product and pride in a job well done is a fertile field for the PR specialist. Taking the 'product' as anything from a manufactured article to a particular service, the PR department has the well understood role of 'selling' it to the public using a variety of communication techniques designed to achieve the greatest impact within the campaign budget. The spin-off from such a campaign on the employee is sometimes overlooked.

The employee, as both a member of the public *and* a participator in the provision of the product, presents the PR department with an extra challenge which, if successfully pursued, can result in a higher degree of motivation and commitment to the organization. In some cases the employee may purchase the product as a daily necessity or a luxury, or it may be a leisure pursuit, or in other cases it may seem very remote like a piece of machinery for a snow-plough in the Antarctic. In every case, however, it is possible to enhance interest and engender a sense of 'ownership' in the final product. The raw materials may come from a part of the world which is currently in the news, there may be references to it in the national press or other media etc; every opportunity should be taken to connect employees with the end result of their work.

The first opportunity occurs at the induction stage of the new employee. Nothing contributes more to creating a sense of belonging than a detailed knowledge of the 'output' of their new workplace. Publicity material of all kinds including video or audio-visual presentations, can be very effective in this process. It also pays manufacturers and distributors of consumer goods to remember that their own staff are a valuable and close market with built-in advantages. Product pride and follow-on sales from staff recommendations, well outweigh any staff discount allowance. New product sampling and demonstrations in the lunch hour or at the end of the day are usually very popular.

This attempt to build pride in the business is not solely concerned with the product. It also relates very closely to the personalities in the workforce whether in the boardroom or on the shop floor. Any achievement in any area of the organization whether recognition from the Queen in the form of an Honour for one of the directors, or a sporting success by a much humbler member of the staff, deserves prominent mention as a morale factor in bringing people together. Here the house journal, employee report and annual report provide useful channels for conveying the news to the organization as a whole.

4 Participating in the success of the business

A further step up from pride in the organization is the actual sharing of its success in financial terms as an incentive to greater co-operation and productivity. To turn again to Wallace Bell:

It has been shown beyond reasonable doubt that financial partici-pation does have a significant impact on employee attitudes, not least by a survey[2] undertaken in 1983-84.

Of the 2703 respondents in twelve profit sharing companies, 73 per cent said that in their own experience profit sharing improved employee attitudes, and 76 per cent said that it made people take a greater interest in their firm's profits and financial results.

There was no significant difference in the responses to these and the many other questions between managerial, supervisory and general staff, between male and female, trade union and non-union members, or across age ranges. It is interesting, however, that although the survey was made more than two years before the government first introduced proposals for the new 'profit-related pay', a massive 96 per cent said that profit sharing should not be seen as a substitute for an adequate wage or salary.

The positive effect of financial participation on employee atti-tudes is confirmed by many discussions with employees at all levels in scores of companies in all sectors. It is of course not profit sharing or employee shareholding alone that makes the difference. Most profit sharing companies were already participative companies before profit sharing was introduced. Indeed its introduction is usually the consequence rather than the cause of the development of employee involvement processes in other areas – and referring again to Section 1 of the Employment Act 1982 – communication and consultation come before financial participation. That is as it should be.

Against a background of more general involvement practices, however, financial participation can make a critical difference both to employees' interest in and reception of business information, and to their readiness to co-operate with management in improving performance. When everyone shares in the profits, the results become relevant and the psychological distance from the workplace is greatly reduced.

5 Caring communications

Lastly, there are those aspects of communication which are outside the details of the job, outside the concerns of the market and not directly connected with the success of the organization in financial terms, yet, nevertheless, play an important part in integrating the employee as an individual at work and in society as a whole. The contribution of the organization to community projects and to improvements in the environment are important morale factors. A caring philosophy which recognizes the importance of the individual and expresses the objective of developing the inherent talents of every member of the workforce through on-going training throughout their career is likely to provide its own reward in a highly motivated and committed workforce.

References

1   EPIC GROUP. *Industrial relations opinion survey*. London, EPIC, September 1988.
2   BELL D.W. and HANSON C.G. *Profit sharing and profitability*. London, Kogan Page, 1987.

Starting from Scratch

All organizations communicate with their employees, their share-holders and their community. The quality of that communication will vary along the communications continuum. At one end of the scale the information may be minimal, crudely and/or badly communicated, and at the other end of the scale, it may be sophisticated, complex and professionally presented.

In some organizations, communications will be high on the management agenda and on others it will not feature. Professional personnel and line managers will take the issue into their conference rooms and make an objective analysis of where the organization stands. It is then that the quality of their communications begins to improve. In the busy life of most managers, the communications debate may seem so basic as almost to be a waste of time. Yet, without analysis, it may well be that a company's communications performance has stumbled along – just getting by – and failed to make a significant contribution to the business success. Communications can always be improved.

The secret and measure of a manager's strength and success is how to implement action and improvement in this area where everyone is their own expert, and where getting by has, and continues to be, almost acceptable. The cost of getting by is, however, expensive, and fails to secure employee commitment and help managers to manage more effectively.

The first step in any communications analysis is to be objective in assessing the organization's current performance:

- Is the organization aware of who their audience are?
- Is what the organization believes it is communicating, what the audience wants?
- Is what the organization believes the audience want, being communicated well?

These seem to be fundamental starting points from which the manager should work.

The role of PR in the guise of the recruitment advertising agent who will help with house style and develop the corporate image in local, regional or national press and labour markets, is now reasonably well accepted by personnel managers. Larger organizations will see house journals as a legitimate area to involve PR specialists just to keep things looking reasonably professional. But how many organizations have yet taken on board the value of total professionalism in communicating, covering the verbal presentation skills, the myriad of written communications, and the informal, as well as the formal communication structures in their organization?

How many managers would allow a book-keeper to present the company's final financial statement? The acknowledgement that published accounts must be of the highest professional standard goes without question, yet many organizations allow the 'winning of hearts and minds', which, as defined in these pages is the core objective of the communication process, to be left to the *ad hoc* approach of the untrained, overburdened manager.

The need for a written and agreed policy statement on communications may be regarded as a sensible first step from which to progress.

The analysis of how the communication process is being conducted can be done by the Personnel or PR specialist or by an outside opinion research organization, employers' association or other independent body such as ACAS, etc.

An objective and well conducted opinion survey or audit will establish just how much misunderstanding the organization has about its communication performance. In simple terms – if one accepts that personality is not as you are but how others perceive you – then the organization's personality may be quite a different thing from how it is, or wishes to be, or indeed wishes to portray itself to be.

Such a survey might cover not only the employees' perception of the organization's personality, but also how it is perceived by the community, customer or market. It may be important for organizations to have a high acceptance amongst special interest groups – ecology circles, trade unions, financial institutions, or local schools and colleges.

However, most organizations will not be totally unaware of the temperature amongst employees and other groups and a step-by-step review cannot fail to have major advantages in the continual process of improving communications. An audit will either confirm the views already held, or give new ideas for improvement.

No-one really starts from scratch, but *where* one starts from may not be as clear as the organization originally thought.

Assuming the organization has established 'who the audience is', 'what the audience wants' and 'how well the organization is doing it', then the challenge of improving the quality of what is being communicated becomes critical to progress.

There is no simple solution, but the recognition that progress in communications, as in all other management areas, requires the setting of realistic and clear objectives which will be regularly monitored, is a long way forward. A comprehensive blue-print is not possible, but a check list of questions such as 'are they relevant?' 'are they too much?', 'are they too little?' could establish formal communication measures in areas such as:

- The actual job
- Organization and structure
- Working practices
- Relevant competitor performances
- Department performance
- Terms and conditions of employment
- Short/long term business strategies
- Training and development policies
- Market place/competitor performance
- Business results (eg sales, profit and loss, asset base, cash flow, costs, added value)
- Technological developments.

The methods to improve in all of these areas, are well known and listed earlier in this publication. Which particular method to use, is a matter of management judgement that will depend not only on the manager's personality but also on the organization's culture and history, its size and its commercial strength. Traditionally, the weaker the commercial strength of the organization, then the less sophisticated the methods of communications used – 'we can't afford all that time and money' has been the usual response. Whilst acknowledging the commercial reality, the question which should be asked is 'when is the greatest need to communicate effectively, and when do we *really* need to win the hearts and minds of our customers, employees, and communities?' The response may well be that the greatest improvements need to be made when commercially the organization is at its weakest. The need for top management commitment and vision is essential if the organization is to achieve the improvement of profit through professional communications.

Changing with the Times

The accelerating rate of change in the 80s with its privatizations, mergers, organizational restructuring, new systems and new technologies coinciding with the development of new communication techniques, presented management with both the need and the means to change attitudes.

Many of the changes were necessary for economic survival and at the same time there was the fear that the trade unions would impede and stultify the progress necessary to match the efficiency and productivity of competitors abroad. As Nicholas Jones states, in his book *Strikes and the Media:*

> 'Some senior industrial relations directors believed that a strategy for communicating directly with the workforce was the only way to improve competitiveness and speed up the introduction of new products and work practices. They had found that their employees were not always being given an opportunity to understand or adapt because local union representatives controlled the channels of communication. The traditional machinery of trade union consultation could be used effectively to block change, but the new techniques would ensure that employees received the facts directly from those employed to manage and motivate them.'[1]

And gradually, as management chose to strengthen the responsibility of supervisors and foremen, to train senior staff in the skills needed to communicate to groups of workers and to use methods of direct communication with each individual employee, the PR role expanded. Again, to quote Nicholas Jones:

> 'Employers began to rethink their whole approach to both internal and external communications. In previous years state-owned industries and major private employers had used their public relations departments largely to influence public and parliamentary opinion, as they had not seen the same need to devote resources to the task of conveying

information to their workers. Once the pace of technological change quickened and major restructuring became
necessary in order to survive, managements realised that
they had to find ways to counter trade union resistance:
external relations were no longer the sole priority. In some
cases the "public relations director" was replaced by a
"communications director", who was responsible for both
internal and external communications systems. The techniques which had been built up by the public relations
industry were slowly transferred and applied to communications with the workforce. Some employers moved
quickly to take full advantage of both the expansion in radio
and television and the improved services which were being
offered by other traditional means of communication.'[1]

At British Leyland (BL), Sir Michael Edwardes' two-year recovery
plan entailed the complete or partial closure of thirteen factories
with the loss of 25,000 jobs. To achieve this in the face of determined and protracted trade union opposition, the BL management
showed how newspapers, radio and television could be used – and
exploited – to help secure a fundamental change of attitude among
the individuals comprising the workforce:

'The central objective for BL was to get the company's
message across as effectively and as quickly as possible.
This meant acknowledging the importance of the early
evening broadcasts on radio and television. A news item
transmitted at tea-time could give BL an opportunity to
speak directly to the car workers as they drove home from
the factories, or sat down for their evening meal and
watched or listened to the news. The company wanted to
ensure that whenever possible they heard the latest announcement at first hand from the chairman at a time when
it would have maximum impact, not only on the workers
themselves but also on their families, who might be watching or listening too. An equal priority for management was
to make contact with the workforce before local union
leaders had a chance to hold a mass meeting.'[1]

Here is an example of the media being used to change attitudes
under a very positive, management-led initiative. The initiative may
come from other directions such as trade unions or shareholders
when a company is on the receiving end of a takeover bid, as in the
case of Pilkington.

From the moment BTR's bid for Pilkington was announced in the winter of 1986, there was a two-month period of great uncertainty during which the company was rarely out of the media. While the headlines tended to focus on developments in the City and on the drama of demonstrations against the bid by the unions and the local community, the role of the personnel department was less public, but just as crucial.

The group personnel department covered not only the 6,000 employees on its 'home' site at St Helens (almost a one-company town), but 8,000 other employees in the UK at over 70 different sites and 39,000 overseas at 27 locations in 15 countries. To handle the communication problem arising from the hostile bid, the company set out five main objectives:

- to keep all employees aware of the publicly available information on the bid and to get the latest news to them within half a day of its publication
- to be in a position to answer employees' queries and to tell them about their personal situation
- to be able to respond quickly to pension inquiries from former employees
- to maintain open communications with employee representatives
- to maintain open communications with the local community.

Meeting these objectives 'meant setting up a round-the-clock international news agency, using the combined resources of the personnel and public relations departments'.[2] At the start of the campaign the director of personnel and the public relations manager established day and night contact points with the personnel directors of the seven UK divisions and the executives responsible in Europe and elsewhere in the world. The main means of communication used was the company's group bulletin system:

'Normally these are posted out, but for the duration of the takeover battle all the stops were pulled out to make sure that they reached every site within half a day. Where they were available, fax or telex were used; for other sites, cars or motorcycle despatch riders were brought in; if all else failed, the contents of the bulletins were dictated over the phone. To keep up communications with the local community, St Helens' town hall was designated as a "site" so that senior councillors would receive news at the earliest opportunity.'[2]

As it was clear that the main source of fresh developments was the City, a small team (including the company chairman and some other directors) was established in London to lead the City end of the campaign. Using specially installed telecommunications links, they passed the latest news to St Helens which was then 'flashed' to all the established contacts in the UK and around the world.

In addition to the group bulletins, briefing groups were set up, special issues of the group newspaper were produced and a 10-line phone service was installed which employees could call to hear a recorded summary of the latest developments. A 'news room' was set up at head office to display all the published documents, press cuttings and transcripts of television and radio coverage. Copies of all the cuttings and transcripts were then sent to every site. The success of these methods may be judged from the fact that by the end of the campaign these amounted to 'no fewer than 650 pages'[2] and that the phone service attracted around 1,000 calls a day.

The main aims from the management point of view was to ensure that employees understood the mechanisms of the bid and that they did not find out from the media what the predator, BTR, was doing before the company had an opportunity of putting its own case. They also had to put across the message that there might be periods of unavoidable silence due to the Stock Exchange regulations.

In addition there was the need to keep the employee representatives in touch with the situation. The task of communicating with them was made easier through the spontaneous formation of a campaign group of representatives from all divisions, including non-union members. In the words of John Gillespie, the director of personnel.

> 'It was a very responsible group. They kept to the issues of the bid and the reasons why Pilkington should remain independent, with no talk of other companies' records or of government policies. But they also established themselves as independent of the company. Over the years we've had our fights and we've had reductions in labour, so they clearly didn't see us as entirely benevolent – it was more a case of "better the devil you know" . . .'

The success of BL and Pilkington demonstrates the undoubted power of controlled PR, in very different circumstances, to achieve particular ends. Whether the PR role is handled by a PR specialist, the personnel director, or a combined communications team is a matter of internal management preference and will vary from one organization to another, but the overall strategic control must remain vested in management.

In this time of rapid change the PR role is undoubtedly expanding and increasing in importance but there are also dangers of its over-use and possible misuse. A recent report by David Drennan referred to the 'managing' of employee communications, as if expectations of employees can be deliberately raised or lowered to ensure their general acceptance of changed circumstances:

'The beauty of "managing" expectations is that, inevitably, you are forced to manage in advance. Many managers in traditionally unionized industries find themselves pre-occupied with resolving disputes, handling grievances, heading off problems and generally keeping things going. This, of course, is all part of the manager's job, but if managers confine themselves only to managing the present, they will always find themselves managed by the circumstances rather than the reverse. To gain control permanently, their horizon must take in some of the future as well as the present. That is the difference between managing expectations and simply managing industrial relations.'[3]

The principles for managing expectations can, it seems, be orchestrated in a carefully calculated way to achieve the desired impact on the employee by controlling the timing and release of the news at appropriate intervals. This gives managers a powerful tool to handle human relationships, and on occasions there must exist a thin border-line between sensitive communication and news manipulation. It is at this border-line that the closest co-operation between PR and personnel practitioners is called for; the PR function tending to be used by management – with an eye on the 'bottom line' – to secure a particular end result, and the personnel function operating more continuously as a guardian of the integrity of information. This is an over-simplification, as both PR and personnel need to be aware of this inherent dichotomy and work together as a team to ensure due weight is given to each other's role.

References

1 JONES N. *Strikes and the media: communication and conflict.* Oxford, Basil Blackwell, 1986.
2 TURNER D. 'The Pilkington experience'. *Personnel Management.* July 1987
3 DRENNAN D. 'How to make the bad news less bad and the good news great'. *Personnel Management.* August 1988.

Crisis Communications

This section examines the interaction of personnel and PR communication functions in different types of crisis. The first part looks at the employee-centred crisis arising through disputes which have a high level of public interest. In the second part the crisis communications covering major unforeseen events are examined.

Part 1

A different aspect of PR emerges when considering crisis situations caused by strikes and other forms of workplace protest. Industrial relations problems are news, and events of this nature attract immediate, and often unwelcome, media attention. Even small issues can make a splash in a local paper while major company disputes become national headlines.

In the past, the personnel manager was generally infected by the 'no comment' syndrome and consequently it was not felt necessary for senior managers to be trained in handling the media. Terry Ball, writing in *Personnel Management,* describes the situation:

'When I first went into personnel management, I was advised in all seriousness that the role of the media in industrial relations was wholly malicious. We may have had some progress since that time but often a major objective of a personnel manager in a strike or tribunal is to prevent the news reaching the press. Why? Is the terse "no comment" likely to help the organization's case? Will the personnel manager's refusal to come to the phone help in presenting the case to the public?'[1]

Nowadays it is generally recognized that both parties – journalists and personnel managers – need each other in a more positive and professional inter-relationship. As Martyn Melvin put it in a recent article, 'Clearly the personnel manager with an industrial relations problem does not need bad press coverage to add to the difficulties,'[2] and goes on to suggest a number of vital steps which need to be taken to contain the situation:

> 'Appoint someone to handle press enquries and ensure that everyone involved knows who that person is. For preference it should be someone not directly connected with the negotiations, so that they can be available at all times to deal with queries. The public relations manager, where one exists, is the obvious choice.'[3]

Apart from this development of PR as a specialist agency to handle the media, there has been a marked tendecny to use communications techniques to win the battle for the employee's mind in the face of militant trade unionism. Nicholas Jones, in his recent analysis of communication and conflict, traces this development:

> 'Many of the industrial disputes of the late 1970s and early 1980s saw the emergence of strong managements which were determined to persuade strikers to return to work. Trade union leaders found themselves being bypassed by sophisticated techniques which had become available through the modernization and expansion of traditional channels of communication. When faced with difficult industrial disputes, instead of relying on the expertise of their own industrial relations department, employers turned increasingly to consultants in the communications and advertising industry, who had developed new ways of taking advantage of the postal and telephone services. Several of these consultants were to become the closest advisers to the chairmen of nationalized industries and major companies as well as to the government. The techniques deployed by management included extensive advertising in national and local newspapers; personal letters from the chairman to the home of each worker; recorded telephone messages giving employees advice on how to break a strike; and sometimes opinion surveys among the staff which were carried out in secret and used by management to help work out policy objectives. Some disputes saw the full panoply of such counter measures in use.'[4]

This new practice of negotiating through the media has been seen in most of the major disputes of the 1980s – British Leyland, British

Rail, the Coal Industry, P&O Ferries etc – in each, the employers and the unions concerned have tried to influence the news media and take the communication initiative. The media in turn, in a battle fought out through the newspapers, on radio and television as much as on the picket line or the shop floor, has influenced the conduct of management and union leaders.

As Nicholas Jones points out:

> 'What has been so crucial is, that during major stoppages, the government, the nationalized industries and other large employers have tried to devise a communications strategy, a strategy which can assume considerable significance during long disputes.'[5]

Management has taken the lead in setting the agenda and made maximum use of the media, instead of waiting for the media to come to them. The problems of co-ordinating the strategy between the PR and personnel specialists at these times of high tension are considerable although of enormous importance in the long-term effect on the organization.

In these crisis situations involving the giants of industry with anything from 100,000 to 200,000 workers spread throughout the country, the full range of communication techniques are being brought into play in an effort to influence the result. Radio and TV interviews, letters and bulletins to employee's home (aided by computerized records), freefone service, advertisements in free newspapers and in the local and national press, are all now regularly used by both management and unions. However, it is generally management, through the use of professional PR consultants, that succeeds better in dovetailing its communication strategy with its industrial strategy, for example:

- the British Rail letter from the chairman, Sir Peter Parker, in June 1982, to each member of staff and posted to their homes, with these emotive sentences under the heading 'You, your family and your job' –

  'It is now one minute to midnight. Unless commonsense from ordinary railwaymen takes over, the railways are now due to start the most disastrous strike in their history.'

- the British Leyland press releases to the newspapers which were synchronized with the more direct channels of communication by arranging short 'spontaneous' interviews with the chairman, Sir Michael Edwardes –

' A typical ploy of the PR department was to tip off TV and radio newsrooms: Sir Michael would be prepared to stop for a minute on his way out of the office and would have something to say. TV crews and radio reporters should wait at the top of the exit from the underground car park in Portman Square. Sir Michael would emerge, often doing no more than wind down the car window. He would have his say, and perhaps answer a question or two. But once he had made his point or felt the questions had gone far enough, he would wind up the window and drive off.'[5]

- British Coal's use of full-page advertisements in the Sunday newspapers combined with articles contrived to ensure maximum coverage by the Secretary of State, Peter Walker and the Coal Board holding a series of exclusive briefings with Sunday journalists throughout the strike –

- the P&O Ferries' use of full-page advertisements in the national newspapers to press home the almost irresistible logic of their case (see figure 1 page 60).

The use of advertisements is a new phenomenon and not confined to management; in the rail guards dispute in 1985, British Rail spent an estimated £8 million on press advertising and the NUR, appreciating the need to communicate with the public before embarking on any strike action, responded by its own advertisements explaining and justifying their case for retaining guards on passenger trains. Such powerful campaigns with budgets running in the £ millions must be viewed with some concern if communications during industrial disputes are not to deteriorate into public mud-slinging matches. There is a practical problem to face up to, that those who have the information – such as the authoritative daily figures of miners returning to work – have opportunities to manipulate the media by the timing of their press releases. As Nicholas Jones points out:

'The distinction between propaganda and news is often not as clear-cut as critics of the news media would have you believe.'[7]

Peter Riddell of *The Financial Times,* when quoting the comments of the chairman of the Independent Broadcasting Authority – Lord Thomson – on the increase in government spending on advertising, wrote:

I SEE NO NEED TO MODERNISE UNREALISTIC WORKING PRACTICES THAT ARE CRIPPLING THE COMPANY

I SEE NO THREAT FROM FOREIGN COMPETITORS WHO DON'T SUFFER FROM THE SAME OUTDATED WORK PRACTICES THAT WE DO

I SEE NO CHALLENGE FROM A CHANNEL TUNNEL THAT WILL OFFER CUSTOMERS AN ALTERNATIVE TO SEA TRAVEL

When Nelson turned a blind eye to the dangers ahead there was something heroic about it.

When a trade union does so, it's plain madness.

Because the realities of trying to run a business won't just disappear.

Time and again we explained this to the NUS leadership but they wouldn't see it.

Fortunately. the majority of our workforce did. 65% accepted our offer of between £11,000 and £17,000 per year with up to 243 days off.

An offer that experienced seamen are currently queueing up to accept.

At some stage the talking had to stop and we had to get on with running a ferry business.

If we hadn't, a few years from now, there'd have been no ships to see.

'I SEE NO SHIPS

. . . at least, not British ones

Figure 1

'Lord Thomson said the Government was using
"the persuasive and visual skills of advertising agencies to a
degree which governments didn't do in the past. This
change brings the risk of transgressing the line between
objective information and making a party political point."
The IBA has apparently insisted on changes in certain
recent advertisements.'[8]

This exposes the difference of approach between PR and PM
specialists already referred to in earlier chapters. In order to 'win'
the dispute, PR strategy tends to concentrate on public opinion and
likely employee waverers in such a dramatic and effective way that
journalists, as Nicholas Jones confesses, are 'often swept along by
management hype'. However, much of the efforts of personnel
management are concentrated on restoring normal harmonious
relations after the return to work. This only emphasizes the need to
co-ordinate the PR/PM activities in the long term interest of their
organization, and the importance of maintaining the integrity of
news values.

One idea towards achieving this end was mentioned by Geoffrey
Goodman, when industrial editor of the Daily Mirror, in an article
on redressing the balance of inadequate media reporting:

'Why not a widespread experiment within factories with
closed circuit TV information units? In large companies
with plants dotted around Britain, a TV information network would offer an invaluable link especially if it were
made available to unions and management jointly.

Or why not industrial newspapers on a more imaginative
and more independent basis than the usual "company
hand-out"? I have long been an advocate of the independent industrial newspaper, financed out of company funds
(perhaps with a trade union contribution) but with editorial
control vested in a kind of independent trust appointed (or
possibly even elected) by management and unions. This
would provide much greater credibility than the routine
company newspaper: there would be a check on any
irresponsibility; the paper would not be dependent either
on the chairman's veto or the shop steward's whim; it would
be independent of external "market" forces; it would offer
a platform to anyone within the group wishing to air a view,
however controversial or absurd, and it would always be
answered.

My own view is that this form of newspaper will eventually develop and flourish throughout most of our major industries. There are already several examples of this idea in existence such as the Port of London Authority's fortnightly paper, *The Port*.

The point I am making and will go on repeating, is that at least some of the remedy for our "media problem" lies within the grasp of industry itself.'[9]

In the meantime, until the gap between the dream and the reality is narrowed, here is some sound advice from Martyn Melvin on how PR and PM specialists -- however their duties interface in the particular circumstances of each organization – should respond to the press during disputes:

'Anticipate what the press might want to know. Prepare a statement which is factual, unambiguous, not too long and not inflammatory or defamatory. Work out well in advance exactly what message you want to put across. Remember, you are trying to fill a vacuum. If you don't fill it, someone else will, and it won't be in the way in which you or the chief executive would like.

Decide whether you want to issue a press statement or wait and reply to inquiries. If you issue a statement, be very careful that you get the timing right. Telling the press something before telling your employees is not recommended.

When a statement is read to a journalist over the phone, always ensure that it is read back to check that it is correct.

Instruct everyone that no one except the designated "press officer" should talk to the press; *all* inquiries should be channelled to that one person.

Keep the press officer up to date as things progress, and go through the statements together in detail. It is vital that the press officer sticks exactly to the agreed statement and is not led to answer other questions. Ad-libbing is dangerous. However experienced the press officer, if they are not directly involved in the proceedings, they may unwittingly say the wrong thing at a crucial time.

If you are going to be interviewed, have a practise first, with a colleague playing the part of the journalist.'[10]

The final message that comes through when considering crisis communication, is the importance of improving the often neglected training of directors and senior managers in handling the media so that they will be in a better position to develop a coherent strategy which co-ordinates the two essential and complementary arms of PR and personnel management.

Part 2

When a crisis comes, communication is one of the most effective tools in damage limitation.

There have been many examples over the past few years which demonstrate the value of a well-oiled communications machine swinging into action when the need arises, or, conversely, the adverse reactions that are generated by poorly handled communications.

Negative responses externally also have a significant impact on a company's employees. Seeing their company openly criticized through the nation's media causes confusion and demotivation – particularly when all communication effort is directed at fighting a defensive campaign and employees are left to draw their own conclusions from the media.

The world's worst nuclear accident at Chernobyl was a classic example of a communications void leading to suspicions of a sinister nature. The Russians admitted their mistakes and acknowledged the additional damage caused to their relations with the West by lack of communications.

Speaking at an international conference in Melbourne two years after the accident, Professor Yassen Zassoursky, dean of the faculty of journalism at Moscow University said:

> 'We are to blame that we didn't let people in the world know what was happening and that included the neighbouring nations. It was only two weeks after the explosion that a press conference was called to try and make up for some loss of credibility.'
> 'We were not good at communicating and this delay meant a lot of speculation in the Western media . . .'

> 'Chernobyl was not just a local accident. It was an international tragedy which involved a sort of trial of the Soviet Union.'

> 'Chernobyl provided a hard lesson for the Soviet Union. But we have learned from our mistakes, and have now set up a special PR and information unit at the plant.'

British Nuclear Fuels at Sellafield initiated a campaign to exploit the benefits of pro-active communications, without the spur of a disaster. Public concern and ignorance were enough to prompt them into establishing a sophisticated, high-profile information centre at the site which has become one of the leading attractions in the area with many thousands of visitors every year.

Being ready to deal with a crisis with a detailed contingency plan is an essential discipline which many companies still fail to adopt.

They may have planned how to deal with the problem itself – like the logistics of re-calling potentially contaminated food – but few have precise communications plans with clearly designated roles and responsibilities in place.

There were contrasting media reactions to the corporate response following the Townsend Thoreson Zeebrugge disaster and the Piper Alpha tragedy.

Townsend Thoreson was slammed by the press for its inadequate information facilities. The company allegedly defended the accusation that its switchboard was jammed for seven hours, blocking flow of information, by explaining that the BBC had given out the press office telephone number instead of the relevant police station for worried relatives to call. Meanwhile relatives were reported to be clamouring for news at Dover with only two press officers vainly attempting to cope with the sheer size of the operation.

Townsend Thoreson insisted afterwards that it had an effective crisis contingency plan to deal with potential disasters but the additional criticisms they faced, and the inevitable hostile media reaction, highlighted the faults in the plan when it was put into action.

The information process triggered by Occidental International Oil to deal with the Piper Alpha disaster was subsequently described as a 'textbook' case of crisis communications management.

The company's press office had begun operations just 14 minutes after receiving a telex about an 'incident' on the oil rig. A holding statement went out immediately and the first of many press conferences was held within minutes. A team of 35 office staff with special training in crisis management were seconded to a special unit, fielding media calls round the clock on a shift basis.

During that time the Minister of Energy had gone to Aberdeen and given two press conferences and Armand Hammer, Occidental's President, had flown in from America and was talking openly and honestly to the media.

Nothing could detract from the inevitable media post-mortem that Occidental had to face, but they were not subjected to the 'mauling' that companies less open in similar situations, have suffered.

Any organization can find itself unexpectedly caught up in a hostile media campagn, particularly in the public sector where the press see their role as 'watchdog' for morality.

Take Cleveland, for example, where in June 1987 a routine council debate on a problem in their social services department concerning young children, was reported in two local newspapers. Within a week it had escalated to front page features in the *Daily Mail,* becoming the biggest and longest running news story of the year – now commonly known as the Cleveland child abuse controversy.

Cleveland's PR department operated the usual press cutting service and within the first five weeks over 9,000 cuttings accumulated, with daily mentions on national TV news. The media, to quote Robin Treacher:

> 'was determined to do two things – report anything and everything with a child sexual abuse link and out-do any competition. They went to incredible lengths. Apart from a general judgement bias, it involved editorial blackmail (give them what they want or they'll print something really nasty), an invasion of council offices, misleading telephone calls (the PRO said an officer could talk – when it certainly had not been agreed), camping outside social workers' houses, breaking confidentiality agreements during the search for a missing social worker who had left a suicide note, and publication of confidential high court evidence.'[11]

The agonizing position the PR staff found themselves in, was that while they were expected to co-operate, assist and be as open as possible with the media, they were prohibited from telling the council's side of the story owing to the need to respect complete confidentiality of parents and children.

As the campaign progressed the PR team developed the technique of staging every second of media exposure so as to prevent the council side of the story being media led.

The action taken to ensure this vital objective included:

- a tight restriction on who could talk to the press. Answers to difficult questions were circulated among this group

- during the busiest period there was a daily briefing for key players

- modules were prepared covering anticipated questions

- press conferences were carefully staged and statements scripted in advance, making sure pre-press conference briefings did not turn into management meetings

- a refusal to agree to TV or radio interviews until it was known who the interviewer would be, and whether the council spokesman would be part of a panel which might include protagonists with an unfair advantage.

The lesson learned was to plan ahead, integrate the organization's approach to communication and always try to keep the media initiative.

Conclusion

Managers in medium and small organizations may feel that the scale of the crises depicted here is so enormous that there are few lessons that apply to their situation. Yet there is always the chance of a fire, a robbery, food poisoning, etc, on any site, whatever the size, calling for the same communication response – to employees and to the media.

References

1 BALL T. 'Do we get the media we deserve?' *Personnel Management*. December 1984.
2 MELVIN M. 'Personnel in practice – back in the headlines'. *Personnel Management*. April 1988.
3 ibid
4 JONES N. *Strikes and the media: communication and conflict*. Oxford, Basil Blackwell, 1986.
5 JONES N. *The media and industrial relations: the changing relationship*. Warwick Papers in Industrial Relations. No.15. November 1987.
6 ibid
7 ibid
8 RIDDLE P. 'Tory advertising raises concern'. *The Financial Times*, 9 May 1988.
9 GOODMAN G. 'The impact of the media on industrial relations'. *Personnel Management*. October 1979.
10 MELVIN M. *op cit.*
11 TREACHER R. 'The problem with being in the media'. *Local Government Chronicle*. 22 July 1988.

Sub-Contractors Dimension

Throughout this book, management's responsibility to communicate with their employees has been stressed, yet this misses an important factor: what about those on site who are not employees in the legal sense, such as contract workers, maintenance firms, agency staff, certain part-timers and the self-employed? They are a growing group – covered by the new term 'peripheral workers', as opposed to 'core-workers' – who have important information needs of their own.

Many employers today are quick to point an accusing finger at earlier managers who allowed the communication channel to the shop floor to be monopolized by the shop-steward yet, in historical terms, in relation to labour, the shop-steward was in some ways carrying out a similar function as the modern contractor and employment agency. Gang working with casual labour not signed-on as individual employees, left the negotiation of rates and payments to the shop-steward who became, quite naturally, the main channel of communication.

The employer may have no legal duty to negotiate and communicate beyond the main contractor, but it would be prudent to ensure that each individual person working on site, regardless of their employment status, receives essential and updated information about the job, safety, smoking, no-smoking rules, first-aid, canteens, etc. The so-called 'peripheral workers' may be in the same union as the permanent employees, with the risk of being involved in each other's disputes, of not crossing picket lines, of sharing in an industrial relations balloting constituency and so on, making it more important than ever to include them in any communications message.

On occasion the 'peripheral-workers' may be leading the communication field, with inside knowledge of new buildings and machinery on site before the permanent staff are aware of the changes in store for them. Outside suppliers too, may have prior information through the tendering process, particularly in the public sector, and their delivery drivers will often bring with them disturbing rumours of pending developments. There are other contract workers who are often as permanent as regular employees, such as canteen and catering staff, and by virtue of the personal contact in their job have a close identification with the employees and the organization. Whoever is designated responsible for communicating with such groups needs to appreciate the sensitivity of staff who may well regard themselves as employees and part of the organization.

Many examples could be given where the integration of communication between outside and inside staff has not taken place, with unfortunate results. Here is one typical incident:

Contract lorry drivers delivering raw materials to a manufacturing unit were asked by their employer to comment on changes to their shift patterns to allow delivery of different and greater amounts of materials to the factory.

The fact that this might mean that some of the process departments in the factory, which had traditionally made these materials, would no longer be required, was soon communicated by the lorry drivers and both local management and employees were instantly aggrieved and united to oppose the changes.

The clear message is that the communication policy needs to include all types of workers in an integrated information network.

Public Sector Dimension

Throughout this book care has been taken to use terminology which would be as appropriate to the public sector as the private sector – hence references to 'organizations' rather than 'companies' – the underlying principles of effective communication being common to both. However, there are some distinct factors or combination of factors in the public sector giving rise to communication problems which need to be tackled in a way untypical of the private sector.

Those factors which influence the type of communications strategy adopted in the public sector were set out in the Institute's recent publication, *Employee communications in the public sector*[1] and can be summarized as follows:

1 Size

The huge numbers involved – seven million employees or a third of the entire employed workforce – and the cost of communicating with them with public money, imposes limitations on what can be done and does much to explain the adoption of formalized communication structures.

2 Fragmentation

A split into hundreds of separate geographical units spread over a county, region or even the entire country – eg county councils, such as Kent with nearly 900 locations – raises special difficulties of ensuring contact, consistency and control.

3 Diversity

A complex of employment categories and representative bodies – 58 recognized trade unions for local authority workers, 40 in the National Health Service – causes considerable communication problems and makes it that much harder to distil common corporate objectives.

> 'The information that a police officer needs about the employing authority and its aims may vary considerably from the needs of a social worker or teacher. The diversity has an impact on the method of communication that is chosen . . .'[1]

4 Working arrangements

The different (or much greater) use of part-timers in the public sector compared to the private sector – one in seven in public administration, nearly two in five in education and health services – can greatly increase the cost in time and effort of communications. The problem is compounded by requirements for a continuous seven-day week, 24-hour day cover; very different from the traditional shift arrangements of private industry:

'The use of part-timers working odd hours to meet these short-term needs adds to the difficulties of communication'[1]

5 Politicization

There is an additional dimension, particularly in local government – that of elected members – which calls for some differences of emphasis:
'the organization's objectives must recognize management's statutory responsibilities and any accountability to an elected body and ultimately to an electorate. The position of customers is also less straightforward: they may be beneficiaries of services, or those who pay for them, or both; but as such, their relationship with the organization is just as crucial as it is in a commercial firm.'[2]

This political element is reflected in trade union attitudes, with personnel managers in the public sector sometimes finding themselves 'drawn into disputes of no relevance to their own organization', with 'formal consultative and communications procedures used as a vehicle for political posturing rather than effective two-way discussion of matters of common interest.'[1] The elected members also tend to get in on the act and encroach on the traditional management field.

In order to overcome the special problems arising out of this unique combination of factors, the public sector tends to place a different emphasis on many of the generally accepted channels of communication.

The *written* channels cover everything from notices, letters to employees, briefing notes, bulletins, newsletters, house journals, annual reports and employee handbooks. The public sector slant on these can be seen in the following quotations:

Notices

'In the Civil Service a great deal of communication, both
internal and external, is in writing. . . . at departmental,
divisional or local level, there are ways of staunching the
daily flood of paper across desks. It is possible to experiment with ways of targeting paper better: for example,
similar items can be grouped together and distributed as
bundles or bulletins, with contents clearly flagged or in-
dexed; notices can be saved up for weekly or fortnightly
rather than daily distribution. Local managers are in the
best position to say what are the essential items of paper,
how often they should be distributed, to whom and in what
form.'[3]

Letters

'Management-produced letters to employees have increased
in popularity recently in the public sector as they are a useful
way of conveying information on a single important topic'[1]

Briefing notes

'. . . some system of parallel communications should also
exist for managers . . . Too often, public sector managers
wait for the official notice from on high about the result of
the pay settlement and their own employees have to find
out what has been agreed either through the national press
or through the union representatives.'[1]

House journals

'Many government departments and other bodies have
house journals, ranging from typewritten newsletters to
tabloid newspapers to glossy magazines. Content, fre-
quency, and costs also vary widely because departments
have tried, as far as possible, to tailor the style, size and
presentation to meet the needs of the audience. Many have
carried out surveys to assess staff needs and preferences
before making changes. In some cases, journals concentrate on communicating management interests. In others,
more is made of social and sports news and events. Some
departments put control into the hands of an editorial or
advisory board, although day-to-day exercise of editorial
judgement normally rests with the editor.

Other departments which have launched new house journals, or extensively remodelled old ones, in recent years include: Department of Trade and Industry; Cabinet Office; DHSS; Lord Chancellor's Department; Government Communications Headquarters; Public Record Office; Export Credits Guarantee Department.'[3]

Annual reports

'It may be thought that financial information for public sector employees does not have quite the same relevance as in the private sector. In fact the annual report is an ideal place to bring together all the information disseminated over the year regarding the five "Ps" (progress, profitability, plans, policies and people) along with some estimate of the future.'[1]

'Most major – and many smaller – government departments produce annual reports; in some cases there are statutory requirements to report on specific activities. . . . In 1986 the National Audit Office (NAO) recommended that all departments should produce annual reports, including information about their aims, objectives and achieved performance. The NAO also commended the efforts being made to improve the presentation of Government reports, including the use of graphics, different typefaces and colours.'[3]

The *oral* channels cover mass meetings, department meetings, briefing groups, quality circles and courses and conferences. Again a distinct public sector approach can be detected, due to having a highly fragmented and decentralized workforce. Many meetings would, in a number of cases, be inappropriate and even departmental meetings ineffective:

'A number of personnel managers in the public sector have reservations about whether their often elaborate communications structure really gets the message across to the average employee. This was particularly so if the employee was working in a group based away from the local depot for much of the time. In the transport sector, for instance, management noted the great difficulty in communicating effectively with bus drivers and conductors or with train crews. In many of the utilities field employees work largely in groups of two from home and comparatively rarely report to their depot.

Some organizations have therefore sought to bring the medium of verbal communications down to groups below the level of departmental or unit meetings via the process of briefing groups. Most of these have been introduced under the guidance of The Industrial Society.'[1]

Audio-visual presentations represent a third channel of communication which is gaining in popularity in the public sector, particularly as a means of getting over a message aimed at a specific group where consistency of information is of prime importance. However . . .

'Against these advantages management should also consider the problems, particularly those of cost and time. A full audio-visual system is very expensive and, because of this, is generally a limited resource which means that it can take weeks or even months for the message to reach all employees.'[1]

No one particular means of communication suits all situations and, as in the private sector, a combination of methods – written, oral and audio-visual – will often prove the most effective but the mix of them in the public sector is likely to be significantly different.

Finally the question arises as to who is the person or authority responsible for communications. In the public sector it is less easy to identify the traditional personnel role for corporate and external affairs. In the Civil Service:

'A number of departments have either appointed a full-time communications officer or given the responsibility to a particular officer along with other duties –

eg *Exports Credits Guarantee Department.* Following a communications survey in 1985, . . . appointed a Departmental Communications Officer (who) reports to the Head of Personnel Management

or communications committees or groups –

eg *Home Office.* In November 1985, the Home Office set up a Standing Group on Communications between management and staff . . . to report to the personnel management sub-committee from time to time on the committee's progress.'[3]

In conclusion, an example from the same source brings home the lesson of how good communications are an integral part of every manager's job and the particular difficulties that sometimes have to be overcome in the public sector:

Ministry of Defence (Royal Navy Dockyards)

The two naval dockyards, at Devonport and Rosyth, employ some 18,000 people and have an annual turnover of about £420 million. In July 1985 the Government announced that following a review of naval work it was proposing to introduce legislation to put the dockyards under commercial management. The trade unions were strongly opposed to the move, which made good communications between management and the workforce all the more important. Hay Management Consultants had been called in earlier by the chief executive of dockyards in anticipation of significant changes to dockyard operations.

Hay found that the trades unions and local media were considered by the workforce to be a more credible source of information than local management. Existing methods of communication with the workforce, through monthly dockyard newspapers and a weak cascade briefing system, were not effective enough to support a major programme of change. Hay worked with MOD managers to devise a communications strategy and also helped train thirty key MOD people in media work.

Communications strategy

- All those affected should be properly and promptly informed of the proposals in detail and how they would be affected

- Dockyard managers should explain the programme of change on managerial grounds

- MOD must be the prime source of information for all interested parties

- Arrangements should provide access to information, not just more paper

- The Dockyard Planning Team should take the lead.

Action

1 The issuing of a ministerial statement followed by a letter to all employees at home

2 A series of presentations at the yards

3 The introduction of topical weekly/fortnightly bulletins – produced in-house on two sides of A4 paper handed to employees by individual managers. Each bulletin takes two man-days per week to produce

4 Production of "Annual Reports" at Devonport and Rosyth, setting out operating targets for a two-year period against which progress can be reported quarterly in the local bulletin.'[3]

References

1 PERKINS G. *Employee communications in the public sector.* London, Institute of Personnel Management, 1986.

2 INSTITUTE OF PERSONNEL MANAGEMENT and INDUSTRIAL PARTICIPATION ASSOCIATION. *Employee involvement and participation code.* London, IPM/IPA Rev. ed 1985.

3 CABINET OFFICE. *Getting the best out of people: a guide to improving communications and the involvement of staff, based on experience in government departments.* HMSO, 1987.

The European and International Dimension

The principles and practices of communication advocated elsewhere in this publication are equally true when employee communication is placed in an international context. Likewise many of the warnings remain valid. The detailed examinations of what one is trying to achieve, the culture(s) within which one is communicating and the most suitable mechanics to ensure the success of the process, do not really change. The fundamental differences lie in the complexity of international politics, the variety of national backgrounds, the more complex processes, and probably most important of all, in the person doing the analysis having enough understanding of other countries and the effect of distance and time to view the subject on an international plane. The leap in complexity is such that one must really be sure of the purpose and the value of the exercise before embarking. It must always be remembered that it is difficult to turn communication off and on like a tap – once started, a train of events is set in motion which cannot easily be stopped or reversed and expectations are created for the future which one must continue to meet, if credibility is to be maintained.

As employee communication is the product of company culture, in essence company culture must supersede regional or national culture and become the unifying element in helping a business or a group of businesses achieve required goals. This is a tall order, given that both the subsidiary business culture and local culture are likely to oppose such a trend. It does mean that one has to develop very clear aims in a limited number of areas and ensure that in these areas an international culture prevails, whilst allowing local autonomy and local culture to predominate in a large part of the remaining activities.

The requirement for an international culture is, therefore, only valid where the organization or its markets are of an international nature; where success in achieving objectives is enhanced by drawing support from other geographical areas; where doing things in a particular way throughout an organization adds strength to that organization; and where the creation of a 'family' in some way adds power to the business. Not all businesses fit such a pattern, and it may well be best for their subsidiaries to have separate and overtly linked existences.

However, if all or some of the above issues are important, then *the purposes* of international communication can include the following:

- to reinforce group culture so as to improve the speed and effectiveness of decision taking
- to encourage information exchange in internationally related activities and prevent the 'reinvention of the wheel'
- to form the background to the succession planning activity – certain cultures demand certain types of people
- to establish in peoples' minds what is expected of them by the parent company
- to facilitate change in a way acceptable to the parent company
- to undermine the 'not invented here' attitudes and thereby encourage changes
- to improve the attractiveness of the company in the recruitment field – particularly where the subsidiary is small and far from base
- to encourage small activities, which may be tomorrow's 'cream', and give such activities a perspective within the international activities.

However, like everything in life there is a price to be paid. An intensive international communication exercise may bring together people, ideas, circumstances that one might prefer to keep separate. The sense of local belonging might be weakened and give people the view that a higher authority exists to which one can appeal when unhappy with one's local lot. It might strengthen the 'family' ties with business which one may not wish to retain without the portfolio, and of course there is a cost attached to the exercise.

In summary – there are often good and valid reasons for carrying out an international communications activity – but the benefits must be weighed against the disadvantages. It is not something that should be done just because it is a 'nice' idea – it is too costly an activity in time and money for that approach! It is something that is only done when clear and valid reasons are established.

However, having decided to go ahead, the issue of competing national cultures has to be faced.

First, the culture issue will be used by all those wishing to remain 'autonomous' as a reason for not co-operating. Anyone who has worked in this field knows how often one is told – your ideas may be valid in your country, but they cannot work here because of our different national culture, legal system of business claims, etc.

On some rare occasions, the above might be true. However, in most cases this will not be so – business concepts, and people's reactions to business situations do not fundamentally change in moving from one country to another. However, if one does not take care it is easy to create enough cultural issues of a general nature to destroy the communication process. For example, it is particularly easy for the parent company to look at matters entirely through the perspective of one country and almost introduce a feeling of 'new colonialization'. The UK, and in particular a certain type of English background, seems very prone to this criticism. After many years in the common market how many UK companies refer in their reports, notices etc to the UK and Europe – as if those were still quite separate? Then in the next breath, they are quite prepared to talk about North America, South America or Australasia! It is all a matter of increasing one's sensitivity to such issues. Should Australia always be at the bottom of the map? Why not from time to time turn it upside down and place Europe on the fringe? When information is sent out is it in the language of the receiving country – and that can include American English! The headquarters itself is often the worst culprit in not testing communication by the simple experiment of saying 'If I were receiving this document how would I feel?'

There are other pitfalls to be avoided in this area of culture and communication. Translations have to be good – not just correct – but good in style. The tone and style of any message must match the level of understanding of the people receiving it. One has to recognize that different countries have different value systems and will judge messages against these values. If messages are loosely worded, then local interpretation will be 'fed in'. One has to avoid inadvertent communication, eg missing out something which is then seen, far from base, as an important signal.

Some examples which have been encountered, include:

- the reaction in France, when a company went to great lengths to describe the beautiful rural setting of its factory, was – 'they look on us as country bumpkins'

- the New Zealander, who quite seriously extolled the value of the 'upside down map'

- the Canadians who felt that they had as much to contribute back to base, as base had to them but had no apparent way of doing so

- the real puzzlement in the United States over some common English phrases such as 'swings and roundabouts'
- the annoyance of a small number of people in Holland who did not appreciate the explanation that they were not a large enough group to have communications in their own language – Dutch
- the complaint from the United States where the ages of people in the pictures looked discriminatory – ie all young
- the story from the Middle East where pictures of females doing traditional 'male' jobs was not greatly appreciated

Of course the process is simpler in purely western or western type countries. Once one moves outside these areas one can have accusations that:

- the life-style being portrayed is alien
- the politics are alien – eg some political systems view business as being about creating employment, not improving productivity
- and most important of all, the comment that 'few of our workers can read'.

The best advice on this whole matter was probably given by Robert Burns – 'O wad some power the giftie gie us to see oursels as ithers see us!'

Nevertheless, international companies are meeting a growing number of issues on which they have to communicate. This may not only be a difficulty but may also be an opportunity. It is probably easier to communicate internationally on specific issues, for example, health and safety, than on more philosophical issues. The amount of ambiguity is reduced and culture issues do not easily arise if one is communicating the need to do a particular task in a particular way. People may not like such direct communication – but that is for the more ordinary reason that they like to be independent – rather than because of any danger of ambiguity. Messages extolling greater effort, or a particular management style run a greater risk of not being understood.

The single European market in 1992 and free trade between the United States and Canada, forecast to grow over the next few years, will both add a dimension to the communication field. We already see in Canada that language/cultural discrimination is a very real issue, and one not likely to be less important as minority languages (either like Spanish growing in the United States or French declining in proportional terms in Canada) defend their 'corner'. Looking at the changing shape of legislation in Europe being brought about by moves to a single market in 1992, communication and cultural issues could well become not only significant issues – but issues on which a lot of time and effort will be focused. For example, under the freedom of movement of labour legislation, will large groups have to advertise their internal vacancies Europe-wide, if currently they do so in part of Europe – particularly if that part of Europe is where the headquarters and ownership lies? Will company reports have to be produced in the languages of all the employees/shareholders expected to read the reports? Will a social report such as that being produced now in France and Holland become essential for all European businesses and will this again have to be multi-language? Will other social policies such as health and safety, employee benefits, employee participation etc now be trans-national not by choice, but by law? Even if the above matters do not come to pass by legislation, will it aid employee commitment/performance to do such things on a voluntary basis? As yet we may have seen only the tip of the iceberg on this subject, and a by-product of 1992 in Europe may be a communications explosion for multi-national companies. An interesting point is that for the first time perhaps, those driving the communication/culture issues from a nationalistic point of view will be going in the same direction as the commercial interests; for example, to function effectively a single market must learn how to overcome its different sectional interests and components by recognizing their right to exist and by dealing with them as equals. This will give a real boost to Europe-wide communication initiatives, particularly in large companies.

With regard to the mechanics of international communication, of course one uses all the normal methods, for example, newspapers, videos, cassettes, posters, slides, displays, 'teach-ins'. Therefore the comments that follow are more about some practical issues.

First, dealing with language – translators should always work into their own 'mother' tongue. Moreover, it should not be assumed that because people are of a particular nationality their written language is good or their technical knowledge is sufficient. One would not make such assumptions in one's own country or language, and therefore should not take it for granted in another language. More subtle, is to check, for example, English against American or Australian, otherwise some real misunderstandings can arise. The same is true, for example, of different types of Spanish and between French and French Canadian.

With other languages there is often the added difficulty, not only of dialects, but also of writing. Most difficult of all, it is not always easy for the producer to check the accuracy of what has been translated; quite an act of faith!

In the past we have tended to think mostly of the written word, but with the growth of video and slides there is a new dimension – for example, how best to overvoice an original tape done at head-quarters, into other languages. Here it is necessary to pick suitable voices for the images and to decide whether or not one should also hear the original language.

All of the above has two good effects. It often sharpens up the quality of the original text, removing many ambiguities. It also favours the use of more diagrams, photos, or illustrations, which are international in their meaning – and this can be a considerable improvement for everyone.

Secondly is the question of dealing with time. The combination of hour changes between countries, plus the actual time taken to transmit information, makes this a difficult issue if one wants a fairly simultaneous announcement of important information throughout a world-wide group. New systems of fax and courier have helped. However, the great danger now is getting things issued *on* time – it is difficult retracting information or preventing communication if one has changed one's mind. The lesson is – be sure you are ready and happy to communicate when you 'press the button'.

The next consideration is the communication system. Most organizations have tended to grow in odd shapes for fairly obscure historical reasons. These tendencies are often even more exaggerated in the international arena. Resistance to communications is increased if the organization's sensitivities are overlooked. However, if one pays too much attention to the politics, nothing is ever communicated – either because it doesn't get through the chain of command or because it is so out of date when it arrives it is worthless. There is, therefore, a great need to get the actual distribution systems for communications well organized, clearly understood by those using them and running like 'clockwork', as each occasion arises. The organization of communication channels may often not match the company's organizational structure. Tidiness is not the aim. Getting the message through quickly without treading on too many toes is the objective. The aim should be to get any information produced and distributed within a matter of days rather than weeks.

In a way, the above leads naturally to the next point. It is helpful if the person responsible for issuing communications, has enough authority and understanding to ensure action is taken on information 'quality control' and distribution, without the need of committees or too much consultation. Using the 80/20 rule, it is often better to get information out rather than wait until it is 100 per cent perfect.

Another issue is that of the relevance of the information being distributed. When one is far from base one passes a different judgement on what is important. It is essential for corporate credibility that people feel that what they receive is actually of value and importance – otherwise it looks like a large exercise for nothing. This leads to concentrating on shorter messages, less frequently – but messages which are apparently worthwhile. This, then, has the advantage that one can insist that the information is passed on.

To avoid the charge of colonialism and to satisfy local sensitivities, as much scope as possible should be built into the system to allow local 'tailoring' – provided of course the main message is not altered or the quality reduced. It also helps to give plenty of opportunity for feedback and sharing of ideas.

Sometimes it is really hard to look at situations through other people's eyes. Classic in this situation is the concept of export or defending against 'foreign' competition. Exports to one part of an international group may be imports to another part. Who is foreign?

Another common difficulty along the same lines is to believe that people know enough about each others' countries or products to make sense of what is being described. For instance, to anyone living in St. Louis, USA, the town of Union is probably quite well known. However, the location is not so apparent to a New Zealander or an Indian or a European. The same is true of products. Simple maps, photographs, diagrams all help spread understanding.

Courses in foreign languages and cultures can be a great help in overcoming many difficulties – not simply because of what is actually learned about the subject – but because it helps those taking part, to view life from a new perspective. This is probably most important at corporate headquarters as it helps jolt people out of their 'rut'.

Amongst the other ways of building international communication are the use of formal organization 'needs' meetings and training. In the former, the requirement to announce half year and annual results can be built into a major communication exchange cum social event. Likewise exchanges between businesses in the group making the same products, or working parties on product or market developments can play their part.

On a more extended basis, the actual transfer of people between companies in different countries as part of their career development, can be very beneficial both to them and to the company.

The social event, which helps to foster individual links should not be under-rated. It is often a powerful tool at an individual level and helps break down barriers.

In the course of training, multi-national courses can be of great benefit to improved relationships and networking. Likewise, the input to courses, if properly geared, can help change everyone's perspective. If training can include the presence of the key international figures in the company as speakers, dinner hosts etc, it can be even more effective in re-enforcing a common philosophy.

One last caution. In some countries, certain communications are often closely monitored by law. For example, in Quebec it is illegal to post any notice in English to more than three people unless a proper French translation is attached. In the personnel field this problem is compounded by legislation on health and safety, contracts of employment etc. In Belgium, for example, there is a legal framework covering the question of who should receive company information and in what order of precedence. Nothing pleases local unit management more, in its search for national self-esteem, than the headquarters getting themselves in some legal muddle – even when it is quite possible the locals wouldn't have known any better!

Hence to the last piece of advice. In this activity, one must constantly ask for help, consult local management and *listen* to the replies being given. One may have to act in a different way to what local management might wish – but at least the decision will be taken with knowledge of the issues.

All of the above concentrates on the need or otherwise to have 'international' communication in a multi-national company, and where the need is established, to look at the mechanics and possible pitfalls. There is one other issue relevant to this publication; where should the responsibility lie? There is, quite naturally, in the field of communication, a large overlap between the personnel function and the public relations function (provided of course that either or both exist!). There is no doubt that the further a business is from the headquarters, the less it distinguishes between functions and the more it classes everyone as 'head office'. In these circumstances, heads of businesses will tend to deal with whoever they have met and know. It may seem to some organizations that a convenient line can be drawn between anything primarily directed *internally* which should be the responsibility of the personnel function and anything directed *externally* which should be public relations. However, this is an over-simplification. Where, for example, industrial disputes start to affect the wider community – investors, customers and suppliers – then the internal and external messages have to be in line. This is often true in respect of announcements about acquisitions, investments, establishment of new operations or large-scale redundancy or closures. The communication on all these issues may have to be led by the personnel function. However, close liaison has to take place with those responsible for public relations so that one-off 'incidents' don't undermine months, or even years, of careful image-building outside the business. The contrary is also true. High profile publicity aimed at the outside world can be very important. It should, however, be remembered that it is likely to be available for internal consumption (a growing issue now that employee share ownership is much more common) and, therefore, has to be carefully timed and vetted so as not to upset any internal balances.

Internationally, amongst the key issues are those of time and timing. Really good channels of communication must exist between the two functions so that units don't get bombarded with what appears to be conflicting messages over a short period of time. It follows that it is essential that both functions have the same understanding of the group's culture. In essence, so long as each function appreciates that it does not live in a separate world, but that the two worlds interact and overlap, then one is well along the road to harmony. Indeed, the impact of one world on the other should not always be viewed as negative. The key phrases have to be mutual understanding, co-operation and co-ordination.

To summarize, international communication should follow the same principles and apply the same good practices as any other kind of communication. It is the complexity of competing cultures, mixed with people's natural desire to be independent, which create the more difficult issues. Provided it is clear that there is a real purpose and that proper limited objectives are set, it is on the mechanics of international communication that most time has to be spent. This can become a very specialist activity or at least an activity where the person responsible requires a lot of experience, much sensitivity and the unusual ability to sit outside his or her own culture.

All the signs are that this whole area will become a key activity in multi-national companies.

3. Examples of Good Practice

Case History 1
IBM UK Limited
Integrated communications philosophy in action

Background

Analysis of continuously successful companies reveals that two main ingredients are a sound business/people philosophy and good communications.

IBM is a noteworthy example where good communications through both personnel and PR channels is an integral part of a sound business/people philosophy and indeed of a total, and continually evolving, organizational culture.

The IBM approach to employee relations is founded on the basic belief of respect for each employee as an individual and, as stated in their policy framework, 'to provide a maximum degree of satisfaction on the part of its employees in their assigned tasks'. It is not altruistic since IBM acknowledges that long term employee motivation and commitment is necessary in order to achieve the company goals and these can only be achieved if employees perceive that management pays equal attention to achieving employee goals. This balance of company and employee goals is brought about by developing a close working relationship between employee and manager aided by the stated policy, 'to provide intelligent, dynamic, capable management.' By keeping manager and non-manager ratios low (currently 1:7 on average for IBM UK Limited with its total of 18,000 employees) and by carefully selecting and training managers through regular Management Development programmes (where the planned objective is 40 hours people management training per year for each of IBM's 2,400 managers in the UK) – managers are able to build effective and integrated teams.

These principles together with the following personnel policies are made known to all new employees via an employee handbook, which each receives with the offer of employment letter, and are explained in detail at the induction programme. The personnel policy framework at IBM is decribed under the following eight headings – each of which applies to all of its employees as there are no traditional hourly, weekly or monthly groupings, and all employees have common staff status in these areas. Although all form part of IBM's integrated personnel philosophy based on regular communication and involvement, the last two items are of most direct concern here and are covered in greater detail.

1 Full employment

is a commitment on the part of IBM to maintain continuous employment for all regular employees who perform satisfactorily. Employees are not laid off when business changes occur.

2 Fairness in promotion

primary emphasis for promotion is given to performance, whilst internal candidates are preferred to outside applicants. Associated with this is the annual appraisal and counselling programme which also equally applies to all. This includes performance plans, appraising employees on achievement against objectives, counselling on areas of performance requiring improvement and helping employees set realistic plans for further development.

3 Pay for performance

all employees are rewarded for achievement against annual job objectives, within one integrated salary system. Each salary range is wide enough to accommodate four levels of performance and is based on an annual survey of leading companies to ensure it compares favourably with those paid for similar work.

4 Equal opportunity

applies to all employees regardless of age, sex, marital status, colour, or national or ethnic origin or disability.

5 Common terms and conditions of employment

all employees work the same 37-hour basic week and there is a common entitlement to vacations, pensions, life assurance, travel accident insurance, sickness and accident payments, BUPA coverage discounted shares, reimbursements for moving/home guarantee, internal assignments, etc, all of which compare favourably with other leading companies.

6 No artificial status barriers

all employees use the same cafeteria, the same car parks and the same toilets.

7 Communication channels

regular and close day-to-day contact between manager and employee is crucial. In addition there are numerous channels at IBM that are equally available to all employees. One or more of which are often used to reinforce others. Some are top down, others are the reverse but the whole aim of them all is to ensure that regular, open, two-way dialogue takes place.

Briefing meetings – the chief executive and reporting directors meet weekly and immediately thereafter pass key decisions and messages down the management hierarchy. To support this, management briefing meetings are held every two months for the top 60/70 managers, to report business progress and to stress key messages and intentions. Copies of many of the briefing foils are passed down to all managers for use at their meetings. All employees attend these regular departmental meetings every four to six weeks to hear and discuss this information from top management which is suported, when necessary, by video tapes (eg on financial results) and management instruction letters, which announce policy changes together with explanatory question and answer notes. Employees are also encouraged to raise any other matters of concern or interest to them. To complete the communication cycle the manager is expected to communicate the highlights of these departmental meetings in note form, both up the line and to the personnel department. In this way any concerns are picked up and dealt with at an early stage.

Publications – there is a country-wide newspaper, IBM UK News, published twice monthly, and divisional newsletters for each of the main sites/functions. There are hundreds of notice boards in over 60 locations around the UK, all using the same layout and the same notices, each with the same issue and remove dates so that clutter is avoided and prominence is given to the latest notice. In addition all employees receive a copy of the Annual Review which contains the usual shareholders report and also includes information on demographics, overseas assignments, secondments, earnings, equal opportunities, student and YTS schemes, award schemes and use of appeals procedures.

Management involvement – a number of approaches are specifically designed to ensure top management have the opportunity to hear at firsthand what employees are saying and thinking. These include visits to departmental, branch and functional meetings, round-table lunches and coffee meetings for groups of 15-20 randomly selected employees, and executive 'skip-level' or leap-frog interviews. All of which aim to cut out the filtering that occurs in management chains. In addition there are annual 'kick-off' meetings, for all employees at a particular site, designed to start the year well motivated and thank employees for last year's efforts.

Opinion surveys – all employees are given the opportunity to participate in the regular and anonymous opinion surveys that occur biennially on a divisional basis and are staggered to achieve a rolling morale reading. Consistently over 90 per cent of employees participate. The purpose is to alert management effectively to employee views and to measure attitudes and morale on a wide range of company practices, policies and on management itself. The information is then shared with employees by departmental managers, and used as an aid to developing any action plans that are necessary. Similarly, functional site, and divisional action plans are developed, all aimed at ensuring the highest possible level of employee satisfaction and stability.

Communication surveys – are also held at less frequent intervals. In a sample survey held in one part of the company in 1986, employees were asked to reply to the question, 'What is your best source of information?'. The following table indicates that the manager is the best source of information in many of the key areas and the manager together with the company back-up provided to him, is the best source in all areas. Notice boards, also, are seen to be particularly good in providing 'career opportunity' and 'organization and appointments' information.

These surveys are very helpful in responding to employee needs. The communications (PR) and the personnel functions particularly use them to adjust to changing requirements, and wherever seems necessary, in getting messages over to employees effectively.

What is your best source of information:	Rounded Percentages								
	Manager/Meetings	Notice Boards	IBM UK News – Company Newspaper (2 per month)	Division/location periodical	Video	Management Information Letters	Management Topics Magazines (4 per year)	Casual Sources	No Good Source
1. Strategies and objectives in your part of the Company?	47	15	2	11	2	5	—	14	2
2. Strategies and objectives of the Company as a whole?	20	16	27	5	12	8	1	4	7
3. Progress and achievements in your part of the Company?	33	14	7	32	4	1	—	5	3
4. Progress and achievements of the Company as a whole?	11	19	44	2	11	7	1	3	3
5. Career opportunities?	24	60	—	—	—	—	—	6	9
6. Training and education?	59	16	—	2	—	3	—	8	12
7. Salary policy?	67	2	—	1	2	6	1	8	11
8. Pension plans?	36	4	5	3	4	31	—	6	12
9. Other Company benefits?	33	8	4	2	3	41	1	6	3
10. Basic beliefs?	56	5	5	2	4	4	2	7	16
11. Procedures that affect you?	73	5	—	1	—	5	1	9	5
12. Organization and appointments?	10	72	2	2	—	8	—	3	2
13. IBM products and services?	7	26	35	3	3	7	—	8	10
14. IBM's market place?	5	12	42	3	5	4	—	11	18
15. Key issues facing the Company?	46	10	13	14	9	3	2	2	2

8 Appeal procedures

finally, communications extend to the appeal procedures. Some times issues will arise which cannot be resolved within the immediate framework of the employee/manager relationship. To meet this need, employees can raise concerns in any of the following ways:

Speak Up! is a confidential programme which employees can use in anonymity to make comments about any aspects of the company and receive considered replies from senior management. Those subjects having general applicability are published in the company newspaper.

The Open Door policy allows employees to appeal against decisions which affect them, and to make that appeal at any higher level of management they choose. Resident managers, who are the chief executive's personal representatives in their regions, are available, as are personnel professionals, to provide impartial advice and assistance to employees who seek help in solving personal grievances.

IBM, in summary, sees good communications whether internal, external, personnel or PR based, as a whole and as an integral part of a continually evolving, organizational culture. Each part of IBM's policies, programmes, and practices are designed to achieve the spirit of co-operation that enables it to be the successful company it strives to be. Its employees appear to support this approach as labour turnover is maintained at a low and consistent 3 per cent. Employers see its merits too, as a recent study[1] of 300 company directors shows. When asked 'Which companies are the most progressive at the moment in adopting overall personnel policies?' – their ranking of the final five was 1 IBM; 2 Marks & Spencer; 3 ICI; 4 Shell; 5 Mars.

References

1 DELOITTE, HASKINS AND SELLS (Management Consultancy Division). *The management challenge for the UK: a research study.* 1987.

Case History 2
MSAS Holdings Limited
Acquisition of
Jardine Cargo International

Summary

MSAS Holdings Limited, a subsidiary of UK-based Ocean Transport & Trading plc, one of the world's leading freight forwarding businesses, had reached agreement to acquire the Jardine Cargo International group of companies from its Hong Kong based parent, Jardine Matheson Holdings Limited.

The merger of the two companies would make the combined operation one of the largest in the world and there were concerns about customer and supplier reactions.

International freight forwarding is a business largely built on personal contact and so maintaining staff commitment, particularly within the acquired Jardine Cargo International companies, was regarded as vital to the continuity of the business.

Both MSAS and Jardine Cargo are international operations with a total of 3,100 staff operating from 130 offices in over 25 countries. This presented particular problems in communications, not least because of language and time difference. Within Jardine Cargo International the problem was even more acute because the group consisted of 12 autonomous businesses with no centralized reporting structure.

The communication task was complicated by the fact that MSAS intended to integrate the businesses but would not be able to provide details of how this would be achieved until after the take-over. There was going to be a requirement for some rationalization and the introduction of a new corporate identity phasing out the Jardine name.

Jardine was informed of the intended acquisition less than a month before completion so severe time constraints became a factor.

Objectives

The communication objectives were:

- Initially to maintain confidentiality until a complete communications programme had been developed and could be implemented in a controlled way.

- To ensure that staff of both organizations heard the news first and that the information was communicated face to face in a consistent format.

- Having gained the commitment and support of employees, to involve them in communicating with customers and agents, in their own home territories.

These communications objectives were designed to secure the following goals for MSAS Holdings:

- The commitment of staff within both organizations, despite the obvious uncertainty which the acquisition would create.

- The retention of customers of both businesses throughout the world.

- The support of agents and suppliers.

Strategy

A strategic planning group was immediately formed which consisted of: the chairman, managing director, marketing director and public relations manager of MSAS; a representative from the Jardine Matheson Holdings company and the managing director and account director from the PR consultancy handling the communications task.

After analysing opportunities and risks, strengths and weaknesses, a three phase strategy was devised.

- Announcement phase – low key 'business as usual' message

- Development phase – reassurance and gradual integration

- Re-launch phase – introduction of new identity and creation of platform for future growth

Programme

Announcement phase

An internal 'cascade' communications plan was devised based on providing briefing material from the UK and establishing timetable and responsibilities for face-to-face briefings with all staff worldwide on the same day.

Letters and logistics to inform priority customers and suppliers direct from the UK were prepared and briefing material supplied for management and employees in local territories to inform all other customers and suppliers.

All media releases were to be sent direct from the UK.

Development phase

The cascade network established for the announcement – supported by comprehensive briefing material – was used to communicate the new structure and management responsibilities to staff, customers and suppliers.

Re-launch phase

All the worldwide management were brought together for a re-launch conference. The cascade network was used again to disseminate key messages to the staff, and guidance was provided on local customer and media briefings.

A new corporate brochure was produced to coincide with the conference, and a personal copy provided for all members of staff.

A special conference issue of the employee magazine *Top Cat* was produced for distribution to all staff and customers.

Material and publications to support the briefings were produced in English, French, German and Japanese.

Results

The merger received a positive response from employees of both companies worldwide.

Checklist returns detailing contact with customers, confirmed that an effective, swift communication process was undertaken by the employees responsible.

MSAS experienced no customer attrition from either company, and many customers thanked the company for keeping them so well informed.

The re-structuring and re-launch was successfully accomplished within the timetable.

Media coverage was favourable with emphasis on the new MSAS strengths rather than on its rationalization.

Case History 3
Reedpack Limited
Management Buy-Out

The aim of employee and staff communications during Management Buy-Outs (MBOs) is to engender job security and to assure continuity of leadership – although many debt-laden MBOs sooner or later sell off parts of the whole and trim staffing levels as unemotionally as an asset stripper in order to reduce loan liabilities.

In the early stages of any purchase, secrecy has to be maintained while various suitors put together their bids. Everyone plays their cards very close to their chests – but with teams of accountants tooth-combing through the books and endless meetings where the directors are closeted behind locked doors, it's not difficult for anyone from the gate-keeper to the factory manager to assume that something pretty significant is going on.

In the case of Reedpack Limited – 1988's biggest MBO – Reed International (RI) invited bids for Reed Manufacturing Group (RMG) from one buyer who would keep the group together and secure the future of all 12,500 employees.

At £618 million, RMG's chief executive, J Peter Williams and his MBO team of six financial, personnel and production directors considered they had struck a reasonable price for the nine newsprint, packaging and office supplies companies spread across 83 sites in the UK, Belgium and Holland. However, if they were to keep the group on course to meet business plans agreed a year before RI took the strategic decision to sell RMG, and keep the group together as RI had 'insisted' against the reality of a massive bank debt, then it would be essential for every unit to achieve, or hopefully beat, its business targets from day one.

With a cast of hundreds – solicitors, tax consultants and City specialists – personnel director John Benson set out to create three employee and management share participation schemes to be launched if the MBO bid ultimately succeeded – the theory being that anyone who owns a piece of the action is clearly going to be motivated to achieving the best possible results. Joint ownership would also strengthen the 'family' unit.

In the majority of MBOs, the management team carries all the financial risk – reaps the rewards or carries the losses. Those are the ones you don't read about.

Reedpack's backers – British Rail and British Steel Pension Funds, 3is, the Pru and Globe Investment – insisted that the Board bought over £600,000 of equity, and agreed to a Management Share Purchase Scheme offering a further £1.3 million in ordinary shares and £3.5 million for an Employee Share Purchase programme. They also gave approval to a Share Saver Scheme for everyone on the full-time pay roll that would be introduced within a year of the purchase of the Group from Reed International.

With the framework for shares schemes established, and the contracts exchanged, there was something tangible and exciting to present to management and workforce. The MBO could come out of the cupboard through detailed presentations to 240 key managers who would cascade the news of the planned MBO and its benefits to the workforce. This would certainly reduce, if not take away, the doubts and uncertainty that flourish on any ill-informed grapevine and become a major element in carrying on 'business as usual'. The presentations to management would be backed by a 'no-nonsense' employee newspaper and a video explaining the Employee Share Scheme. In the words of John Benson – 'Our aim was to present the new company almost as an EBO, rather than an MBO'.

What no-one had reckoned with at that stage was a brand new piece of legislative 'wizardry' called the Financial Services Act 1988 brought in to protect the gullible being parted from their cash through promises of untold wealth. And being new – and as yet untested – legislation, it made no allowance for the directors who genuinely wanted to offer their staff an opportunity to buy shares in the newly-formed MBO company – Reedpack Ltd.

In a few brief paragraphs, the Financial Service Act 1988 regulates stringently any communication about share purchase requirements. It required that any written information must carry a liberal dose of Government Health Warnings – 'the value of shares can go down as well as up'.

This imposed serious restraints on the style of open employee communications the management wished to adopt with each proposed message needing to be cleared by the company's solicitors.

Since the opening bid to purchase RMG had been prepared in the first ten days of April 1988, the MBO team was more than ever aware of the potential damage that silence from the Board was causing to morale. The press maintained an active flow of speculation.

Between the acceptance of their offer and the final signing of contracts, the MBO Board decided to take the risk of talking to their 240 senior managers – with no slides or visuals, no printed material for their managers to take away or talk over with their families or bank managers, and definitely no beating of the drum. All that the managers were asked to pass on to their workforce was that a Management Buy Out bid had been made to RI and accepted – but that if a last-minute bidder topped the MBO bid, RI would be duty bound to its shareholders to accept. Although it wasn't much, at least it took away some of the speculation.

With every word vetted by solicitors and tax specialists, material was released to the entire workforce the moment the deal was finalized. On the one hand, the solicitors were dedicated to keeping the Board out of trouble, on the other, the communications consultants were trying every formula of words they could possibly compile to wheedle their way round the Act. Watching them do battle was one of the more light-hearted aspects of the whole event.

On 27th July 1988, the go-ahead was given to print a newspaper to be issued to every employee. First copies arrived at RI House on the evening of 28th July as the final contracts were being signed. The following day, every employee was handed their own copy – in their own language (the new company operates in the UK and the Benelux countries).

The words they *were* able to use were exciting but not emotive – that life would go on as before, including the planned capital investments programme of £300 million, and that the pension rights and working conditions would remain exactly the same. Instead of detail, big headlines were used with lots of colour to create enthusiasm, and enough 'meat' to get the message across, but censored sufficiently well to keep the Board out of trouble. That weekend, Henry Cooper was brought in to make a video that would explain a little more about the Share Purchase Scheme for employees. The video was shown for the first time at a management conference at Gatwick on 4th August – and by the following Monday, every employee had been invited to see the programme during working hours.

For the conference, the personnel department produced a 150 page guide for management, explaining the detail of the Management Share Purchase Scheme, how to raise the cash for the invited investment, what the tax implications would be, and how management should handle the announcement of the Employee Share Purchase Scheme. A 28-page booklet for employees was produced in English and Dutch inviting them to submit their applications and cheques for £80 blocks of shares by post. In comparison, a new name for the company, new letterheads and signage were simple to implement.

And then came the postal strike. A second newspaper was pre-pared, cleared with the solicitors, printed and distributed to all 12,500 employees. It contained a duplicate application form to use in the internal mail system. This was more interesting and readable than the official application form in the back of the formal offer document, so in many ways the postal strike turned out to be a blessing in disguise.

Despite being severely hampered by the Financial Services Act in what they could say to their staff, the video and newspapers engendered considerable enthusiasm and goodwill.

Did the communications plan work? The Management Share Purchase Scheme was oversubscribed and the Employee Share Scheme attracted well over £1 million of investments – an average of £90 for every person employed. The new company is nearing its business target, maintaining its ambitious capex plans and is already looking at acquisitions in its aim to become Europe's foremost packaging, office supplies and paper specialists.

Finally to quote John Benson, the personnel director:

'The tougher the task, the harder your employee com-munications must work. Most of our employees have been with us for more than twenty years. Their skills and knowledge of the business is vital to our joint success. It's imperative that we keep them in the picture at all times.'

'The greatest compliment we've been paid for our pro-gramme came from a chargehand at one of our northern factories. When I asked him what his people thought of our newspaper, he simply said "You don't find any of them in the dustbin". To me, that spells success.'

Case History 4
Digital Equipment Company
Relocation of Employees

Summary

Digital, one of the world's largest computer companies, employs over 7,000 people in the UK, with 2,900 located at various sites throughout Reading, the UK headquarters.

Rapid growth necessitated new office accommodation to allow for further expansion and to relieve overcrowding in Reading.

Strategically, the company did not want to dominate any one area and therefore while, in the long term, the total number employed in Reading would increase to a maximum of 3,500, in the short term, 700 were to be relocated in two new purpose-built centres at Basingstoke and Fareham in Hampshire.

Those affected were chosen because they represented self-contained groups that could operate away from the HQ. A total of three groups were involved, one group moving to Fareham, and two to Basingstoke.

The disciplines involved were highly specialized and therefore it was critical to avoid significant employee losses through the move.

The principle of a move had become the subject of speculation and it was therefore important that a formal announcement was made as soon as confirmation of property deals had been received.

A PR consultancy was appointed to handle the employee communications programme just four weeks before announcements were due to be made. At that stage the relocation plans were known within Digital as the 'Excentralization Programme'.

The announcement and follow-up meetings were to be made in the last week of September, with decisions required by the end of the year, and with the actual move taking place in the summer of 1988.

Objectives

The communications objectives were:

- To maintain absolute confidentiality until a complete internal communications programme had been developed and implemented.
- To ensure all employees affected heard the proposals first and that the information was communicated simultaneously through face-to-face briefings using a consistent format.
- To involve the most senior function head in the initial announcement, with follow-up meetings run by relevant line management within 24 hours to reprise the main information and field queries and, finally, individual meetings to discuss personal circumstances.
- To ensure that *all* employees, including those staying in Reading, recognized the development as one which demonstrated:
  — the success and growth of Digital in the UK
  — positive action to meet today's and future needs
  — benefits to all from easing pressure on space and company facilities
  — the level of help/information etc provided for those who were moving.

These objectives were designed to secure the following goals for Digital:

- To complete the relocation of employees from Reading to other centres within the specified timescale, and with the full co-operation of those affected – and with the support of other employees.
- To reassure all other employees of the company's continued commitment to Reading as a main centre.
- To maintain good relationships with the local community to allay fears about an 'exodus' from Reading.

Strategy

A strategy was devised which concentrated on the following main points:

- Position the moves as a positive step for the company reflected through an appropriate theme for all materials. The theme adopted was Expansion '88

- Provide full and comprehensive details of the new location and the relevant financial assistance at the time of the initial announcement
- Reassure employees of the strategic importance of the new sites, ie being away from Reading would *not* hinder promotion prospects
- Promote the new location as a good place to live as well as work
- Involve families in the communication process by making all materials available for home use. Family visits were arranged and funded by Digital as part of the relocation policy.

Programme

The Expansion '88 materials provided to assist briefings and inform employees and their families were as follows:

- Briefing pack for all function heads and line management who would handle follow-up meetings. There were three variations to take account of different disciplines and intended relocation. It also included the full contents of information packs available to employees for easy reference purposes
- Video outlining the new office venue and broad details about the location. There were two versions – one for Fareham and one for Basingstoke. The videos were available for employees to take home for family viewing
- Overhead slide presentation kit and speech guidelines for briefers – again in three versions
- Employee information pack (three versions) containing details on all the following topics:
  - the reason for the move and benefits to the company and its employees
  - why those affected had been chosen
  - the new office and relevant facilities and immediate environment
  - the relocation policy (allowances and payments)
  - timetable of events
  - details of housing availability and relative prices in the catchment area
  - schools, colleges and nurseries
  - employment opportunities for family members
  - leisure facilities and amenities

— details of doctors and dentists
— local and relevant national transport details
— a range of useful contacts such as water boards, gas boards, libraries, taxis, churches etc.

Results

Those affected were given until the end of 1987 to make known their intent to make the move or otherwise. Alternative employment was an option for those who wanted to stay in Reading.

At the outset Digital set a target of 70 per cent take-up for all those involved in the moves – either to Basingstoke or Fareham.

The actual take-up was over 90 per cent for the two groups going to Basingstoke and over 70 per cent for the group going to Fareham.

Digital's internal communications manager, Paul Dinwiddy, described the communications programme as 'very successful'. His assessment was as follows:

> 'It was well received by management at Digital and has set us a high standard which we will need to match in future relocation projects. More importantly, Expansion '88 has been positively received by those employees affected by the move. I believe the professionalism of the communications process played a major part in an employee's decision as to whether to relocate or not.
>
> The cost of the project was roughly equivalent to persuading an extra 10 professional employees to move. A small price to pay indeed; especially as this does not take account of the general motivational benefit for the company as a result of Expansion '88. Employees not involved with the move also commented on how well it was handled.'

Case History 5
Digital Equipment Company
Reorganization of its field service operation

Summary

Leading computer company, Digital was undertaking a major reorganization of its field service structure in the UK in July 1987.

The target audience was primarily some 2,000 field service employees directly affected by the changes, many of whom would be required to take on new job roles. Consideration was also given to the information needs of other employees, customers and the market generally.

The reorganization had been the subject of a task force study for over a year and leaks of information had led to speculation, uncertainty and anxiety among employees, which was causing an increase in turnover in certain key areas. The code name for the project was 'DRIVE'.

The communication task was complicated by the fact that the company was unable to give full details of the new structure, as the intention was to undertake a phased introduction over approximately two years and the final details would to some extent 'evolve' over that period.

A further complication was that the reorganization involved merging two tiers of management. The support and commitment of those affected was vital to the success of the project.

PR consultants were appointed to plan and implement the communications programme.

Objectives

- To improve employee morale by diffusing negative rumour and speculation about the motives of the reorganization

- To pave the way for the smooth implementation of the re-organization by securing the support and commitment of field service employees, especially those most affected by the changes
- To encourage feedback from employees so that their reactions could contribute to the development of the plan.

Strategy

The strategy adopted was:

- To explain to employees why Digital, as a dynamic, successful company, needs constantly to reassess its operating procedures and react to changing market conditions
- To explain to employees the proposed reorganization and highlight the benefits of the changes to them, the company and customers
- To use the fact that all details had not been finalized, as a positive attribute, highlighting that employees would be able to make a contribution to its evolution
- To ensure that the information was communicated, initially face-to-face, in a consistent manner using established briefing channels and within as short a timeframe as possible.
- To use the 'code' name DRIVE as the theme for all communications materials as it had been associated with leaks of information and would reassure employees there was *not* a secret agenda.

Programme

A two-stage cascade briefing programme was developed based on Digital's existing communications channels. District managers – one of the groups most affected by the changes – were heavily involved in the process of reassuring employees about the integrity of the communication. Following their briefing by senior management, the 11 district managers communicated the reorganization plan to their teams. The programme comprised:

- Briefing packs for speakers including guidance on running meetings, slide presentations with speaker's notes, and a Q&A section to help field questions
- A video demonstrating Digital's track record in successfully responding to market needs and explaining the benefits of the changes. This was used to set the scene at the start of managers' briefing sessions

- Overhead slide presentations in various permutations, geared to the specific information needs of individual audiences, for managers to use in briefing their teams
- Wallcharts to help briefers explain key details of the reorganization plan
- Factfiles for employees to refer to after briefing sessions, including a summary of the presentation and feedback questionnaire
- Audiotapes produced and distributed a few weeks after the briefings to answer key questions raised by employees at meetings and from the feedback questionnaire in the factfiles.

Results

- The Project Drive package is regarded by Digital field service management as the best functional communication yet to their employees. Project manager Jeff Rees commended the package for 'combining an insight into the long-term with some detail of the short-term future'
- There was positive support and commitment to Project Drive at all levels of the organization as a result of the communication. Feedback indicated that it had prompted widespread interest in the future development of the project
- The Drive package has provided a platform for further employee communications as the reorganization plan evolves. The videotape, for example, is still being used to support new Drive communications as well as in induction training
- All cascade briefings were completed in under three weeks and more than 90 per cent of the target audience reached, despite the summer holiday period.

Case History 6
Courage Limited
Major restructuring of its tied house estate

Summary

Courage Ltd undertook a major strategic change in the operation of its tied house estate at the beginning of 1987, transferring 900 of its 1300 managed pubs to tenancy. The pub managers affected were to be offered a six-month transfer tenancy on special terms, leading (with the agreement of both sides) to the offer of a full tenancy on normal terms. The remaining pubs were to stay under existing management, becoming the flagships of the organization and spearheading new retailing developments.

A complete internal communications programme was devised by a PR consultancy, aimed at securing the commitment of senior managers to the plans and preparing them for 'down the line' briefing responsibilities; gaining agreement to the transfer tenancy from those affected and maintaining support and motivation from those who would remain as managers.

Objectives

Courage needed acceptance for the transfer tenancy from at least 60 per cent of those affected to avoid disruption to the operation of its tied estate. There would inevitably be opposition, not least from the National Association of Licensed House Managers (NALHM), which stood to lose a significant proportion of its membership. Those running the pubs that would remain managed were also a key target audience as their continued commitment and motivation were commercially essential.

Strategy

- To adopt the theme 'Enterprise 87' to reflect the spirit of progress the change heralded – both for the company and individuals.

- To emphasize face-to-face 'personalized' briefings for all those affected.

- To provide materials to ensure the consistency of these briefings throughout the organization.

- To produce separate, but complementary communications packages, geared to the needs of both audiences – transfer tenants and managers – highlighting to each the opportunities available.

- To ensure absolute confidentiality until the formal announcement.

Programme

The material produced included the structure and visual support for briefing of senior management together with a 'how to do it' section covering their onward communications responsibilities and procedures. Transfer tenants and remaining managers were to be briefed at 70 simultaneous meetings throughout the country. There were two versions of the material supplied for these meetings – one for transfer tenants and one for remaining managers – which included videos, overhead presentation kits, and personalized information packs containing brochures and other relevant information such as their pub rent and stock valuation and a specially produced *Running Your Own Business* leaflet.

Results

The success of the communications programme was apparent just seven days after the announcement when 94 per cent of managers had accepted the transfer tenancy – despite vigorous opposition and lobbying from their union – and the remaining managers responded enthusiastically to the move. Courage trade projects director, who was responsible for the implementation of the change, said:

> 'Even some of the critics were impressed by the organization and communication that helped make the project progress so smoothly.'

Conclusion

It may be helpful to summarize the main strands of thought that have emerged in the writing of this book.

1 Management's responsibility

The study of the specialist roles of personnel and public relations in handling employee communications has been based firmly on *management* and the *individual employee*. The communication message is essentially from one to the other, and any resultant discussion or debate between one another. Management has the choice to communicate direct or through its personnel and PR support staff, each working towards organizational objectives for which ultimately management alone is responsible. Similarly, the individual may prefer to stand alone or choose representatives, either union or non-union, to make the message more explicit or raise issues more effectively.

2 PR and personnel roles

PR is typefied by particular communication *campaigns*, having a beginning and an end, within budget limits, using selected channels – often innovatory to maximize effect – beamed at the outside world, the corporate whole of the organization, and the individual employee within a family unit.

Personnel communications, on the other hand, are *continuous* and on-going, using channels which have often been mutually agreed with representatives, generally cascading from the top down through the management hierarchy, and particularly providing an opportunity for feed-back.

3 Need for co-ordination

Managers ignore at their peril the personnel and public relations perspectives in developing their communications strategy. Personnel managers are increasingly less able to handle the sophisticated demands of modern PR without support, and PR needs to realize that their campaigns are not built entirely around written and visual techniques – each is interdependent.

In *normal* times, the different aspects of the personnel and PR roles sometimes leads to overlap and confusion, as highlighted in the opening chapter of the book. Such 'disasters' emphasize the vital need for management to 'get the employee communication act together' and ensure effective co-ordination. In times of *crisis,* caused by strikes, accidents or commercial upheavals, the co-ordination of the two specialist communication roles is put to the severest test and usually in the full and unforgiving glare of the public. It is then that the strengths and weaknesses of the organization's policy and strategy on communications are revealed in action. The chapter on crisis communication is one of the most significant in the book, illustrating the emergence of new joint approaches of PR and personnel in situations which are highly topical.

4 Who does what?

As the book has shown, the two specialist communication roles are clearly separate yet complementary, but the PR/personnel responsibility may be carried out in many different ways. The two roles may be combined in one executive, or each held by a manager reporting to the same (or different) director, or there may be a separate communication unit independent of both (or reporting to one or the other). Whatever the particular organizational structure chosen, the two roles are always there and need to be carefully integrated into management's communication strategy and any special communication situation.

5 No blue-print, only general principles

Students and practitioners in personnel management and public relations tend to seek explicit guidance on the respective functions of these two specialisms in the employee communications field. There are, however, no hard and fast boundary lines, no blue-print. Each organization needs to weigh up the general principles in the context of their *own* situation and devise a communication strategy which stands the test of openness and integrity: one that bridges the gap between management and the individual employee, respects the operational imperatives of management and the sensitivities of employees (eg to hear news affecting them *first* before the rest of the outside world) and in a spirit of inclusiveness, uses management and representative channels as well as direct one-to-one communication. No easy task, hence the 'challenge' in the title; and yet it is more than a challenge, it is a business necessity to meet the needs of the future.

6   The future

Increasing the commitment and involvement of employees will be one of the primary issues of the 1990s, and communication is the key to achieving this objective. There seems little doubt that the future will see an increasing shift from communication through groups, to communication to *individuals* direct. This will bring with it an increasing use of PR facilities to reach the hearts and minds of employees, their immediate families and the local society in which they reside. Nonetheless, there will always remain a *collective* employee activity, the usual domain of personnel management, where management depends on mobilizing the consent of the workforce – whether organized through union representatives or not – to persuade it of the need to change within agreed timescales. Inclusiveness, openness and trust in the honesty of the information are the essential ingredients.

Also available from IPM

EFFECTIVE CHANGE

Twenty ways to make it happen

ANDREW LEIGH

Today's managers live in times of turbulent change. They can ignore change, resist it – or **use** it to improve their organization.

In this major new book, the author of the highly successful *20 Ways to Manage Better* has created an invaluable toolkit of strategies, procedures and techniques for achieving effective change. On leadership and commitment, experimenting and tracking, force fields, team building and 14 more vital areas of skill, Andrew Leigh has distilled the wisdom of the experts and produced the incisive, practical advice managers need. The result is a lively, intensively stimulating book for anyone facing the challenges of the 90s.

ISBN 0 85292 412 7

Also available from IPM

Creating a Committed Workforce
PETER MARTIN & JOHN NICHOLLS

Learn the lessons of the British success stories of the 1980s!

How have major companies achieved dramatic improvements in productivity and results? In this perceptive and hard hitting study, the authors go behind the scenes and talk to the leaders in 14 pioneering businesses like Jaguar and Raleigh, Burton and Schweppes. Here they find profound changes reflecting the impact of Japanese and American management; they are also laying the foundations for the resurgence of UK industry and commerce.

ISBN 0 85292 379 1

Improve your People Skills
PETER HONEY

People skills are the key to success, but if you really want to get the best from others, you must learn to monitor how **you** behave. The basic techniques are easy to learn, yet they can soon transform your effectiveness in the workplace, and are explained clearly and concisely in this incisive new book. All the important areas are covered in this A-Z guide including assertiveness; brainstorming; counselling; customer satisfaction; humour; interviewing; leadership; negotiating; tricky situations etc.

'A clear and simple book . . . full of advice on a range of situations which we have all encountered at one time'

Personnel Management

ISBN 0 85292 396 1